Formation for Parish Social Ministry

BECOMING A COMMUNITY OF SALT AND LIGHT

Peggy Prevoznik Heins

ave maria press   Notre Dame, IN

D1089157

Catholic Charities of the Diocese of Wilmington recognizes that social ministry is an inescapable response to our baptismal call. We are privileged to sponsor this work as a broad and practical framework for that response.

Unless otherwise noted, scripture quotations are from the *New Revised Standard Version* of the Bible, copyright © 1993 and 1989 by the Division of Christian Education of the National Council of Churches of Christ in the U. S. A. Used by permission. All rights reserved.

© 2003 by Catholic Charities, Inc., Diocese of Wilmington

All rights reserved. No part of this book may be used or reproduced in any manner whatsoever except in the case of reprints in the context of reviews, without written permission from Ave Maria Press, Inc., P.O. Box 428, Notre Dame, IN 46556.

www.avemariapress.com

International Standard Book Number: 0-87793-990-X

Cover design: Katherine Robinson Coleman

Text design: Brian C. Conley

Printed and bound in the United States of America.

Library of Congress Cataloging-in-Publication Data
Heins, Peggy Prevoznik.
  Becoming a community of salt and light : formation for parish social ministry / Peggy Prevoznik Heins.
      p. cm.
Includes bibliographical references.
  ISBN 0-87793-990-X (pbk.)
  1. Church work--Catholic Church--Study and teaching. 2. Sociology, Christian (Catholic)--Study and teaching. I. Title.

  BX2347.2.H45 2003
  261.8'071'5--dc21

                                                              2003012209

SALT AND LIGHT PRAYER

Send your Spirit upon us, O Lord!
And anoint us for your mission.
Send us, Lord:
To bring glad tidings to the poor,
Food to the hungry,
Shelter to the homeless.

To proclaim liberty to the captives,
Peace to those at war,
Solidarity with the peoples of the world.

To restore sight to the blind,
Hope to the hopeless,
Perspective to those in power.

To release those in prison,
Liberate those bound by fear,
Loosen the bonds of prejudice.

And to announce a time of favor from you,
Lord Most High.
Help us to be salt and light for your kingdom.
Amen.

CONTENTS

ACKNOWLEDGMENTS

As with any community-oriented project, this manual is the result of a community of people who by their various gifts and roles have contributed to its creation. While some players participated on a more clearly defined basis, everyone's part was vital to making its publication a reality.

While I cannot possibly mention everyone here, I would like to begin my thanks with my former colleagues at Catholic Charities in the Diocese of Wilmington. Sr. Joan Hart, SSND, my predecessor as Director of the Division of Parish Social Ministry, helped with the early stages of the original book. Andy Zampini, my successor, provided the time, energy, and enthusiasm to bring this book to completion. Executive Director Allan J. Daul's steadfast support of Parish Social Ministry kindled the enthusiasm for this project. Bishop Michael Saltarelli provided leadership and invaluable support of the social mission of the church. Sandy Clark performed the painful task of transcribing the old text into a technologically current format. Paul Amrhein, my former colleague and long-time friend, helped with the many details of the original manuscript, facilitated many trainings, and as a result helped to shape the current book.

The expertise and insights of past participants and facilitators from across the country also have contributed to this book. Special thanks are extended to a group of facilitators from across the country who, upon Andy Zampini's initiative and invitation, worked together for over a year to review evaluations, share their own experiences, and help revise the manuscript chapter by chapter. I am grateful for the professional expertise of Marie Barry, Staff Associate from the Office of Social Concerns in the Archdiocese of Washington; Laura Libertore, Project Coordinator from the Office of Social Action in the Archdiocese of Cincinnati; and, Kristi Schulenberg, Director, Parish Social Ministry, Catholic Charities USA. I am thankful for the time spent with such wonderful people. In addition, I extend a special thank you to Tara Poling from the Archdiocese of Cincinnati for her pioneering work in the area of the environment and religion, which served as the foundation for the chapter on Care for God's Creation. I extend special thanks to Dan Driscoll, editor and friend, who helped to smooth the bumps on this road.

On a personal note, all of this was made possible through the love and support of my family. Thank you to my parents, Rita and Steve Prevoznik, and my seven brothers and sisters for their faithfulness and example. A special thank-you to my husband, Richard, whose questioning spirit helped renew my own. Most especially, I thank my children, Sarah, Bobby, and Joey, whose very existence has shed a new light on the meaning of the gospel in my life.

INTRODUCTION

In 1993, the U. S. Catholic bishops, faithful to the long tradition of Catholic social teaching, declared that our parish communities are measured not only by how well they celebrate the sacraments, but also by how well they serve the hungry, the homeless, the sick, those in prison, and the stranger. Working for peace and justice, the bishops proclaimed, is an essential element of parish life. In fact, they declared that working for peace and justice is what makes a parish Catholic.

The statement they issued, "Communities of Salt and Light: Reflections on the Social Mission of the Parish," made a profound impact on Catholic parish life. While many important documents on Catholic social teaching have been issued in this century, "Communities of Salt and Light" brought a very practical and workable element to the parish. Parishes could easily use it as a guide for self-evaluation and as an inspiration to do more and be more.

The book you have in your hands is an attempt at making that document even more accessible. The training program contained here has been used for years in the Diocese of Wilmington, Delaware, and across the country. It has gone through extensive fine-tuning over the years so that what you have is as current and updated as it can be.

HOW TO USE THIS BOOK

Becoming a Community of Salt and Light is a guide to your training in Catholic social teaching. Each session is organized around a major principle of Catholic social teaching and a section of "Communities of Salt and Light." (You'll need to obtain a copy of the document.) Each session also contains a section on skill development, so while you are learning the "what" of Catholic social teaching, you are also learning and practicing the "how to" aspect.

The outlines contained in this book are by no means exhaustive. They are meant to guide your thinking as you learn about Catholic social teaching and its implications on your life and the life of your parish. Write in the margins, cross out lines, add your own points, ask questions, note changes you would make, think big, and trust in the Holy Spirit. This is a part of the learning process, and a means to creating a renewed parish and parish leaders.

Keep an eye out for the Web site icon.

Whenever you see it, you will know that there is further information on that topic at the publisher's Web site: www.avemariapress.com. Visit the Web site and follow the links to *Becoming a Community of Salt and Light*. In addition, each session ends with a list of resources to complement the book and the Web site.

The facilitator's guide in the back of the book contains helpful tips for leading each session.

I wish you many challenging, engaging, exciting, and enlightening moments as you move with your parish community through the inspiring and life-changing social teachings of the church.

Peggy Prevoznik Heins

LIFE AND THE DIGNITY OF THE HUMAN PERSON

AGENDA

- Registration
- Prayer Experience: "You Are the Salt of the Earth"
- Course Overview
- Program Expectations
- Break
- Catholic Social Teaching: General Overview, and the Dignity of the Human Person
- Skill Development: Shared Prayer
- Preparation for Session 2: Care for God's Creation
- Evaluation: Written
- Closing Prayer

PRAYER EXPERIENCE
"YOU ARE THE SALT OF THE EARTH"

Call to Worship

Brief Silence

Opening Prayer

Leader: God of our longing, we seek you in the morning and the evening, in our homes and in our streets. We turn to you in our joy and our sorrow, in our certainty and in our questioning. You have called us by name, and we belong to you. Continue to grant us your mercy as we embark on our journey to discover you in a new way. We ask this through Jesus Christ, who lives and loves with you and the Holy Spirit, now and forever.

All: AMEN!

Reading: Isaiah 43:1–4, 7 "I have called you by name; you are mine."

Quiet Reflection

Reading: Matthew 5:13–16 "You are the salt of the earth, the light of the world"

One-on-One: Quietly meet with one person whom you do not know and ask him or her:

1)   What is *one* of your favorite things to do?
2)   What is *one* thing in today's society that makes you angry?
3)   What is *one* motivating influence that brought you to this training course?
   - You will have five minutes to both share your answers and discuss them.
   - In the large group, you will introduce your partner by sharing his or her: name, parish, parish role, favorite activity, public annoyance, and motivation.
   - Then say, "*Let us pray for _____*"
   - Response: "*You are the salt of the earth*"
   - Continue around the circle

Closing Song

Overview of *Becoming a Community of Salt and Light*

Vision: transformation and evangelization through the church's social mission

I. Program Goals and Objectives
    A. Articulate a personal understanding of your baptismal call to work for social justice and identify one role you can assume in your parish social ministry through—
        1. Prayer, faith sharing, and personal reflection
        2. Small and large group sharing and interaction
        3. Evaluation of the training and one's own gifts
        4. Completion of a one-year personal action plan
        5. Presentation of the church's social tradition and teaching
    B. Identify and describe the seven basic principles of Catholic social teaching (CST) and apply them to your parish's social ministry through—
        1. Regular presentations on the basic principles of CST
        2. Ongoing critical analysis of the bishops' 1993 statement, "Communities of Salt and Light"
        3. Small or large group discussion around the specific principles of CST
        4. The identification of resources for and models of practical parish application
    C. Utilize a base of skills that will enable you to work in collaboration with other parish leaders to advance the implementation of the parish social mission as described by the bishops through—
        1. The practice of such skills as: brainstorming, team building, meeting facilitation, communication, leadership development, volunteer recruitment, project planning, and team building
        2. Ongoing, honest evaluation
        3. Practice of one-on-one interviews with parishioners
        4. Role playing and case studies
        5. Completion of parish assessment and one year personal action plan
        6. The modeling of process and discovery over content and lecture

II. Course Structure
   A. Each session will include three basic parts:
      1. A basic principle from Catholic social teaching
      2. Applied theme from "Communities of Salt and Light"
      3. Skill development for leadership in ministry
   B. Program training will incorporate the "Styles of Ministry" model (see p. 16)

III. Course Process
   A. Interactive and Participatory
      1. Grounded in the belief that every person holds a piece of the truth
      2. We listen to and learn from the truth of others
   B. Experiential
      1. Learn by doing
      2. Respect each other's faith, place, experience
   C. Relational
      1. More important than any program is building relationships
      2. Relationships are the foundation of the social mission: our faith is profoundly social

For reflection:
What do you hope to get out of this training? Write down your expectations here. Share them with a partner.

	Catholic Social Teaching	Theme from "Communities of Salt and Light"	Skills
1.	**Life and Dignity of the Human Person** Goal: Introduce Catholic Social Teaching, develop an understanding of its rootedness in scripture, and establish that the foundation for all ministry and action is prayer and worship.	Prayer and Worship	-Listening (ongoing/introducing/summarizing) -Shared prayer: what and how? -Large group discussion (ongoing) -Evaluation: why and how to? -One-on-ones (basic, ongoing) -Discernment of ministry styles
2.	**Care for God's Creation** Goal: Develop an understanding of the evolution in the church's social teaching related to God's creation and its application vis-à-vis the baptized faithful. Develop a greater appreciation for how our lifestyle choices impact the earth and our global neighbors.		-Reflection -Team building -Team development
3.	**Call to Family, Community, and Participation** Goal: Establish the profoundly social nature of our faith and explore its implications.	Preaching and Education; Supporting the Family	-Reflection -Family perspective -Brainstorming -Small group work (ongoing) -Program planning: Identify problems

4.	**Option for the Poor and Vulnerable**
	Goal: Develop an understanding of the church's option for the poor and explore the role the poor play in our lives, our faith, and ultimately, our own salvation.
		Charity and Outreach	-Program planning: -Reflection
			  *Brainstorm strategies -Process evaluation
			  *Set goals
			  *Identify issue vs. problem

5.	**Rights and Responsibilities**
	Goal: Develop an understanding of social structures/systems.
		Advocacy	-Compare and contrast: -Structural analysis
			  *(inter) personal v. structural -Advocacy skills
			-Program planning: -Oral evaluation
			  *Decision making
			  *Feasibility analysis

6.	**The Dignity of Work and the Rights of Workers** Goal: Establish that the essence of justice, that is, the mission of the Gospel, is to build loving relationships.	Organizing and Development	-Scriptural reflection -Volunteer recruitment -Structural analysis -One-on-ones -Community organizing -Personal goal setting
7.	**Solidarity** Goal: Develop an understanding that the transformation of the world will come about by the poor—and that the work for justice is ultimately about seeking solidarity with all God's people for transformation, and explore the relationship between work for justice and spiritual growth.	Solidarity	-Summary and reflection -Facilitation -Leadership development -Full program evaluation -Effective meeting

STYLES OF MINISTRY[1]

The chart "Styles of Ministry" can be helpful in trying to understand the interaction of various social ministries.

Note the axes. The vertical line represents organizational or project goals with "social stability" at one end and "social change" at the other. The horizontal line depicts decision makers, with the elite, or people with power, making the decisions at one end and a grassroots model of decision making at the other.

The two lines form four quadrants illustrating four styles of ministry, all of them vital for a prosperous and caring community.

The most familiar is the one in the lower left-hand corner. The style here is called charity, and the strategy is social service. Many are engaged in this enabling and supporting ministry with people who are hurting. The aim is to assist them through times of personal and/or social and economic crisis.

The upper left-hand quadrant is another familiar arena. The style is contest, and the strategy is advocacy. Many of us who have benefited from the existing system work very hard to reform, or adjust, the system, believing it could benefit everyone more fairly. This is a process whereby the powerful (usually) speak for the powerless.

The third quadrant in the upper right-hand corner addresses the style of conflict and focuses on the powerless representing themselves. Community organizing and development is the strategy here. The style strives for developing grassroots leadership, building a base of power through one-on-one relationships, and maximizing citizen participation in the decisions that affect people's lives. The goal is not only change in systems—policies, programs, or services—but a change in the process of participating in the decision-making, and possible implementation of those systems as well.

Finally, in the fourth quadrant in the lower right-hand corner, the focus is on solidarity—the idea that humans are radically interdependent and that the concerns of one person or nation are the concerns of all people and nations. Solidarity calls all people to overcome barriers of race, religion, ethnicity, nationality, gender, and economic position.

The vision of solidarity encompasses new structures and institutions that work toward global justice and peace. The decision-making is collective; organizing is indigenous; and the process is a slow one of community self-help.

Much can be learned from this chart. For example, most parishes put a lot of energy into ministries on the left side and not as much to those on the right side. This is natural, in part due to time constraints and in part because professional people, accustomed to controlling resources, are inclined to help others adapt to the existing system for short-term, or immediate gains. Needs are met, crises are alleviated, and results are seen. Thus, much of the resources and energy are devoted to the provision of services as opposed to more long-term systemic change.

The right side calls us to presence and solidarity with communities that are hurting—a more difficult thing to do. The right side calls us to different kinds of ministry, such as listening to, learning from, and advocating with people in poverty. It calls us to link people with limited resources to the capital and technical assistance that has bypassed them in the past in order that they may play a role in their own destination. The time frame is much longer and progress is slow.

Instead of being providers of services, we become providers of information; instead of helping individuals adapt to the existing system, we participate with whole communities in societal transformation. The right side represents an arena of ministry often devoid of resources. It also represents a vision of a just society, one in which everyone has access to the earth's abundance and where all have a stake in the social and economic order. But because it is a long time in the making, the ministries of the left side are essential for meeting immediate needs and decreasing the pain and suffering as they arise.

Often these styles of ministry are in tension with each other. An organization focused on social service delivery, for example, has a hard time with leadership that wants to organize, while community developers have a hard time working with leaders focused on reform. The fact is that no style is more important than another. Each style of ministry is essential in addressing the injustices of the world, and each requires its own set of skills, talents, and commitment. It is likely that our individual preference will fall on either one side or even within one quadrant; it also is likely that that preference will change. The task is to learn from each other and work together to create a more just world.

Where are you on this chart? Who do you need to be in relationship with in order to maintain an appropriate tension or balance in your church or community ministerial work?

Styles of Ministry

Advocacy

SOCIAL CHANGE

Organizing

The strategy of advocacy focuses on the powerful speaking for the powerless. Those who benefit from the existing system work very hard to reform, or fix the system, believing it should benefit everyone fairly.

The focus is on the powerless representing themselves through community organizing and development. This involves developing grassroots leadership, building a base of power through one-on-one relationships and maximizing citizen participation in the decisions that affect people's lives.

ELITE — DECISION MAKING — GRASS ROOTS

Charity

Solidarity

The strategy of maintaining, enabling and supporting ministry with people who are hurting. Provides assistance to others to cope in times of social and economic crisis.

The idea that humans are radically interdependent and that the concerns of one person or nation are the concerns of all people or nations. Solidarity calls all people to overcome barriers of race, religion, ethnicity, nationality, gender, and economic position.

PROGRAM GOALS

SOCIAL STABILITY

An Introduction to Catholic Social Teaching: General Overview and the Dignity of the Human Person[2]

Goal: develop an understanding of the church's social teaching originating in scripture and grounded in the dignity of the human person

I. Constitutive elements of the Catholic faith
   A. Scriptural—faith as wisdom
   B. Sacramental—faith as experience
   C. Social—faith as witness

II. Catholic social tradition—origins in scripture
   A. Old Testament
      1. Genesis 1–11 teaches dignity of the human person
         a) **Sacredness**—foundation of Catholic Social Tradition
            (1) This is God's world. All creation—earth, stars, plants, animals, and ultimately, humankind—reflects God, and by its nature, is good.
            (2) Woman and Man are made in the image and likeness of God; we are sacred.
         b) **Stewardship**—foundation of teaching on justice
            (1) God entrusts the world to us and invites us to be "co-creators."
            (2) We have been given all that is good and therefore have the responsibility to care for it: dominion—not domination or exploitation—over the earth; not owners, but tenants and caretakers.
      2. Genesis, Exodus, Leviticus, and Numbers teach community and interdependence.
         a) **Community**—our spiritual heritage is innately communal.
            (1) Scripture portrays human existence as communal in nature (in sharp contrast to present individualistic society).
            (2) From the very first days, a nomad God made common cause with a chosen people: "I will be your God, and you will be my people" (Lev 26:12).
         b) **Interdependence**—by sharing in God's goodness (sacredness), sharing in God's dominion (stewardship), and having been invited to dwell in community, humanity is inextricably connected to one another, the earth, and God.

(1) We become more like God as we seek to enhance all of creation.

(2) Sabbath/jubilee year—a sabbatical (every seventh or fiftieth) year in which the land was to be left uncultivated, slaves freed, and debts relieved; a new beginning equalizing the level of participation in recognition of interdependence of person to person, and person with the land.

3. Prophets teach that faith and justice are intimately linked to the poor.

   a) The quality of our faith is tested by how we stand with one another, i.e., by the quality of justice in the land.

      (1) Where we stand with God will be tested by where we stand with our people.

   b) Measure the character of justice by assessing how we deal with the widows, orphans, and strangers—the people on the edge.

      (1) Primary message of the prophets was not that the people neglected scripture, forgot the Temple, or worshipped false gods, *but* that the people had forgotten the poor, and therefore had forgotten God.

      (2) *Without the doing of justice, God remains unknown.*

4. **Reflection**: What does the following mean to you: *without the doing of justice, God remains unknown?*

B. New Testament—takes the above themes and deepens them

  1. **Sacredness**—in the incarnation, every human being became the brother and sister of the Lord Jesus, a child of God.

   a) By drawing all people into the love of God (Abba, Father), Jesus reinforces the covenant **Community** theme.

  2. **Stewardship**—was reinforced by Jesus' practice and preaching.

   a) In his relationships with public sinners, and in his respect of women, Jesus affirms the underlying goodness of all created in God's image.

   b) Parables reflect wider goodness of all life

  3. The role of the **Poor**—Jesus challenges all to keep our eye on the edge of the circle, on the poor, for God is there.

a) Jesus announces his mission by bringing "good news to the poor."

b) Jesus reveals himself as the center of a new web of relationships—a new **Community**—with the poor as its privileged locus (Mt 25).

III. Catholic Social Teaching (CST)

How does God's love abide in anyone who has the world's goods and sees a brother or sister in need and yet refuses help? (1 Jn 3:17)

A. The four historical phases of Catholic social teaching
1. Response to the Industrial Revolution: 1891–1941
2. Internationalization: 1941–1991
3. Response of the church to the post-industrial society: 1971–1991
4. Pope John Paul II: 1978–

B. The fourteen major documents of Catholic social teaching
1. *Rerum Novarum*, 1891—Pope Leo XIII: "On the Condition of Labor"
2. *Quadragesimo Anno*, 1931—Pope Pius XI: "On Reconstructing the Social Order"
3. *Mater et Magistra*, 1961—Pope John XXIII: "Christianity and Social Progress"
4. *Pacem in Terris*, 1963—Pope John XXIII: "Peace on Earth"
5. *Guadium et Spes*, 1965—Second Vatican Council: "The Church in the Modern World"
6. *Populorum Progressio*, 1967—Pope Paul VI: "On the Development of Peoples"
7. *Octogesima Adveniens*, 1971—Pope Paul VI: "Call to Action"
8. *Justice in the World*, 1971—Synod of Bishops: "Justice in the World"
9. *Evangelii Nuntiandi*, 1975—Pope Paul VI: "Evangelization in the Modern World"
10. *Redemptor Hominis*, 1979—Pope John Paul II: "Redeemer of Humankind"
11. *Laborem Exercens*, 1981—Pope John Paul II: "On Human Work"
12. *Sollicitudo Rei Socialis*, 1987—Pope John Paul II: "Social Concerns of the Church"
13. *Centesimus Annus*, 1991—Pope John Paul II: "The Hundredth Year"
14. *Evangelium Vitae*, 1995—Pope John Paul II: "The Gospel of Life"

C. The seven major principles of CST (each theme will be explored in the corresponding training session), as identified by the U.S. bishops in 1991:
1. Life and the Dignity of the Human Person
2. Care for God's Creation
3. The Call to Family, Community, and Participation
4. The Option for the Poor and Vulnerable
5. The Rights and Responsibilities of the Human Person
6. The Dignity of Work and the Rights of Workers
7. Solidarity

IV. The Dignity of the Human Person
A. The foundation for Catholic social teaching
1. Old Testament and Jesus' mission are built upon these truths:
a) Man and woman are made in the image and likeness of God
b) Human life is sacred
B. Second Vatican Council: "What is the church saying in and to the world?"
1. The role of the church in the modern world is to be the sign and safeguard of the dignity of the human person—*Gaudium et Spes*, 1965, Second Vatican Council.
2. Church involvement in social issues results when the dignity of the human person is threatened. Thus, the primary purpose of parish social ministry is defined.
C. Current social issues, identified by the U.S. bishops, which pose a potential threat to the dignity of the human person:

Food, Agriculture, Environment	Human Rights	Terrorism
Health	Education	Holy Wars
The Economy	Substance Abuse	Globalization
Discrimination, Racism	Refugees	Inner City Life, Rural Life
Housing	Abortion, Capital Punishment, Euthanasia	Regional Concerns: Middle East, Africa, Latin America
Immigration	Family Life	
Arms Control, Disarmament	Mass Media	

1. These issues provide a basis for evaluating candidates for offices.
2. The quality of justice in our country must be measured by how we stand with our people.
3. **Reflection**: Who are the widows, orphans, and aliens of today? Why are they outside the system?

D. Discussion—dignity of the human person
1. What is your personal experience of human dignity?
2. How do you see the dignity of the human person being threatened today?
3. Does this theme relate to the anger discussed during the prayer service? How? Why?
4. How does your belief (or lack of belief) in human dignity affect the way you interact with others in the world? Why?

V. Skill Development: Shared Prayer
Goal: identify basic elements of shared prayer
A. It is in the liturgy that we find the fundamental direction, motivation and strength for social ministry. Social ministry not genuinely rooted in prayer can easily burn itself out. On the other hand, worship that does not reflect the Lord's call to conversion, service, and justice can become pious ritual empty of the gospel.[3]
B. Large Group Brainstorm: Prayer and Worship
1. "Communities of Salt and Light" suggests that social ministry— action that seeks to acknowledge, restore, and nurture the dignity of the human person—must be anchored in prayer and worship. How can you do this in your own life, in your work (both with the parish and in the secular world), and as a parish community?
2. How do you begin to plan shared prayer?
3. What elements do you include?
C. Small Group Discussion
1. Why do we anchor our ministries in shared prayer?
2. What are your experiences of shared prayer?
3. When has it worked?
4. When did it not work?

VI. Personal Reflection: Our Baptismal Call . . .
A. Holy Baptism is the basis of the whole Christian life, the gateway to life in the Spirit, and the door, which gives access to the other

sacraments. Through Baptism we are free from sin and reborn as daughters and sons of God; we become members of Christ, are incorporated into the church and made sharers in Her mission: Baptism is the sacrament of regeneration through water in the word.

Baptism is God's most beautiful and magnificent gift. . . . We call it gift, grace, anointing, enlightenment, garment of immortality, bath of rebirth, seal, and most precious gift. It is called *gift* because it is conferred on those who bring nothing of their own; *grace* since it is given even to the guilty; *Baptism* because sin is buried in water; *anointing* because it is priestly and royal as are those who are anointed; *enlightenment* because it radiates light; *clothing* since it veils our shame; *bath* because it washes; and *seal* as it is our guard and the sign of God's Lordship.

Baptism not only purifies from all sins, but also makes the neophyte "a new creature," an adopted daughter or son of God, who has become a partaker of the divine nature, member of Christ and co-heir with him, and a temple of the Holy Spirit. . . .

B. Individual Reflection: What does your baptismal call mean to you?

Preparation for Session 2: Care for God's Creation

For the next session . . .

- *Read* one of the following: Job 14:7, Luke 12:24, John 4:13–14, John 12:24, or 1 Corinthians 12:12.
- *Reflect* on your reading amidst the quiet of nature (at least 15 minutes).
- *Write* a reflection on your "quiet time with nature" experience.
- *Talk* with one person whose dignity you have difficulty recognizing; get to know that person.
- *Write* a brief reflection on the following:
  How were your own assumptions about that person's dignity challenged?
- *Reflect* on the "Styles of Ministry" Chart (p. 18)
  How does this model of ministry challenge your own views of charity and justice work?
- *Complete* the Human Dignity Quadrants (p. 25)

Advocacy

What are we already doing for the theme of *Human Dignity* in the area of Advocacy?
1.
2.
3.

What else could we be doing?
1.
2.
3.

Organizing

What are we already doing for the theme of *Human Dignity* in the area of Organizing and Development?
1.
2.
3.

What else could we be doing?
1.
2.
3.

Human Dignity

Charity

What are we already doing for the theme of *Human Dignity* in the area of Charity and Outreach?
1.
2.
3.

What else could we be doing?
1.
2.
3.

Solidarity

What are we already doing for the theme of *Human Dignity* in the area of Solidarity and Community Building?
1.
2.
3.

What else could we be doing?
1.
2.
3.

SESSION 1 RESOURCES
CATHOLIC SOCIAL TEACHING

Church Documents

www.usccb.org

800-235-8722

"In All Things Charity: A Pastoral Challenge for the New Millennium"
English: No. 5-358, 56 pp.
Spanish: No. 5-832, 64 pp.

"Sharing Catholic Social Teaching: Challenges and Directions"
English: No. 5-281, 32 pp.
Spanish: No. 5-803, 32 pp.

"Leader's Guide to *Sharing Catholic Social Teaching*"
No. 5-366, 64 pp.

"Principles, Prophecy, and a Pastoral Response" *Revised Edition*
No. 5-433, 52 pp.

Books

Catholic Social Teaching: Our Best Kept Secret, Peter Henriot, et al. (Orbis Books, 800-258-5838, www.maryknollmall.org)

A Concise Guide to Catholic Social Teaching, Kevin E. McKenna (Ave Maria Press, 800-282-1865, www.avemariapress.com)

Doing Faithjustice: An Introduction to Catholic Social Thought, Fred Kammer, S.J. (Paulist Press, 800-836-3161, www.paulistpress.com)

Responses to 101 Questions on Catholic Social Teaching, Kenneth R. Himes, O.F.M. (Paulist Press, 800-836-3161, http://www.paulistpress.com)

Catholic Social Teaching and Movements, Marvin Krier Mich (Twenty-Third Publications, 800-321-0411, www.twentythirdpublications.com)

Catholic Social Thought: The Documentary Heritage, David J. O'Brien and Thomas A. Shannon, eds. (Orbis Books, 800-258-5838, www.maryknollmall.org)

Proclaiming Justice and Peace: Papal Documents From Rerum Novarum *Through* Centesimus Annus, Michael Walsh and Brian Davies, eds. (Twenty-Third Publications, 800-321-0411 www.twentythirdpublications.com)

Web sites

The Vatican, www.vatican.va

Office for Social Justice, Archdiocese of St. Paul & Minneapolis osjspm.org/

Social Justice and Peace, www.silk.net/RelEd/justice.htm

Catholic Resources on the Net
www-2.cs.cmu.edu/People/spok/catholic.html
Access to Catholic Social Teachings, www.justpeace.org
Busy Christian's Guide to Catholic Social Teaching
www.uscatholic.org/cstline/tline.html
Center of Concern, Education for Justice Web Site, www.coc.org/ej

SKILL BUILDING: PRAYER

Church Documents
www.usccb.org
800-235-8722
"Catholic Household Blessings and Prayers"
No. 292-6, 444 pp.
"Scripture Guide"
Catholic Campaign for Human Development
English No. 5-229, 12 pp.
Spanish: No. 5-230, 12 pp.
"A Justice Prayer Book"
Catholic Campaign for Human Development
English No. 5-231, 24 pp.
Spanish: No. 5-232, 24 pp.

Books
Our Prayers Rise Like Incense, Cindy Pile, ed. (Pax Christi USA, 814-453-4955, www.paxchristiusa.org)
Fire of Peace, edited by Mary Lou Kownacki, OSB (Pax Christi USA, 814-453-4955, www.paxchristiusa.org)
Gathering Prayers, Debra Hintz (Twenty-Third Publications, 800-321-0411, www.twentythirdpublications.com)

Web sites
Praying Each Day www.prayingeachday.org/prayersites.html
Catholic Prayers www.webdesk.com/catholic/prayers
St. Anthony Messenger www.americancatholic.org
Prayers of Justice and Peace for Various Occasions
www.justpeace.org/various.htm
Prayers to Saints for Justice and Peace
www.justpeace.org/saintprayers.htm

CARE FOR GOD'S CREATION

AGENDA
- Prayer: "Earth Litany"
- Recap/Overview
  - Assignments
    - How was your quiet time with nature?
    - What did you learn about yourself from your personal interview?
    - How might we challenge our own sense of the dignity of all creation, much as we challenged our sense of human dignity?
    - What did you learn from completing the Human Dignity Quadrants (p. 25)?
  - Recap
    - Last session introduced the social mission of the church and its foundation, our belief in the dignity of each person, and our baptismal call to live out that mission
    - The "Styles of Ministry" Quadrants (p. 18)
    - Prayer and worship as the anchor for all ministry
  - Overview
    - This session will broaden our sense of dignity of life to include all of God's creation.
- Catholic Social Teaching: Care for God's Creation
- Break
- Introduction to the Ecological Impact
  - Footprint exercise and debriefing
- Skill Development: Team Building
- Preparation for Session 3: Call to Family, Community, and Participation
- Evaluation: Written
- Closing Prayer

EARTH LITANY

Call to Worship

Introduction

The "Earth Litany" was developed by the United Nations Environmental Sabbath Program. Part I calls to mind human arrogance and asks forgiveness for the sin of ecological degradation. Part II emphasizes the human role as co-creators with God in restoring the earth community. Part III is a prayer of thanksgiving for all that the earth gives and teaches us.

Litany (p. 31)

Reflection

Which part of the prayer struck a chord with you?

How would you describe your relationship with creation?

BECOMING A COMMUNITY OF SALT AND LIGHT

Earth Litany

I

Refrain: We have forgotten who we are.

We have forgotten who we are

We have alienated ourselves
from God's unfolding creation

We have become estranged
from the movements of the
earth

We have turned our backs on
the cycles of life

Refrain

We have sought only our own
security

We have exploited simply for
our own ends

We have distorted our
knowledge

We have abused our power

Refrain

Now the land is barren

And the waters are poisoned

And the air is polluted

Refrain

Now the forests are dying

And the creatures are
disappearing

And humans are despairing

Refrain

We ask God's forgiveness

We ask for the gift of
remembering

We ask for the strength to
change

Refrain

(Silence)

II

Refrain: We join with God, the earth, and each other

To bring new life to the land

To restore the waters

To refresh the air

Refrain

To renew the forests

To care for the plants

To protect the creatures

Refrain

To celebrate the seas

To rejoice in the sunlight

To sing the song of the stars

Refrain

To recall our destiny

To renew our spirits

To reinvigorate our bodies

Refrain

To recreate the human
Community

To promote justice and peace

To remember our children

Refrain

We join together as many and
diverse expressions of one
loving God: for the healing
of the earth and the
renewal of all life.

Refrain

(Silence)

III

Refrain: We rejoice with God in all life!

We live in all things

All things live in us

Refrain

We live by the sun

We move with the stars

Refrain

We eat from the earth

We drink from the rain

We breathe the air

Refrain

We share with the creatures

We have strength through
their gifts

Refrain

We depend on the forests

We have knowledge through
their secrets

Refrain

We have the privilege of
seeing and understanding

We have the responsibility of
caring

We have the joy of celebrating

Refrain

We are full of the grace of
creation

We are graceful

We are grateful

Refrain

Adapted from the United Nations Environment Programme Environmental Sabbath/Earth Rest Day packet of prayers, stories, meditations, and other ideas for celebrating the Environmental Sabbath. To receive the packet, write UNEP, 2 U.N. Plaza, New York, NY 10017

CATHOLIC SOCIAL TEACHING: CARE FOR GOD'S CREATION

Goal: develop 1) an understanding of the evolution of "Care for God's Creation" in the church's social teaching, and 2) its application vis-à-vis the Baptized faithful

I. Development of Catholic social teaching—toward an ethic of creation
    A. Care for creation is a relatively new concern being voiced in church documents.
        1. The Second Vatican Council was held at the dawn of the western environmental movement and acknowledged the interconnectedness of all creation.
            a) "God destined the earth and all it contains for all people and nations so that all created things would be shared fairly by all humankind under the guidance of justice tempered by charity."—*Guadium et Spes*, #69
            b) Newly identified concerns, such as the health risks associated with pesticide use, were not addressed.
        2. The Second Vatican Council document, *Guadium et Spes*, 1965, emphasized the accomplishments of technology (new jobs, less labor for humans, medical advancements).
            a) "By the work of our hands or with the help of technology, we till the earth to produce fruit and to make it a dwelling place fit for all of humanity; we also play our part in the life of social groups. In so doing we are realizing God's plan, revealed at the beginning of time, to subdue the earth and perfect the work of creation; at the same time we are perfecting ourselves and observing the command of Christ to devote ourselves to the service of our sisters and brothers."
            —*Guadium et Spes*, #57
            b) The potential threats to humanity and all of creation had not yet been explored.
        3. *Populorum Progressio*, 1967, continues to address the role of creation in social development without specifically addressing environmental issues:
            "The Bible, from the first page on, teaches us that the whole of creation is for humanity, that it is men and women's responsibility to develop it by intelligent effort and by means of their labor to

perfect it, so to speak, for their use. If the world is made to furnish each individual with the means of livelihood and the instruments for growth and progress, all people have therefore the right to find in the world what is necessary for them." —*Populorum Progressio*, #22

B. The church begins to link progress with environmental decline.
   1. Pope Paul VI's *Octogesima Adveniens*, 1971, noted that "man is suddenly becoming aware that by an ill-considered exploitation of nature he risks destroying it and becoming in turn the victim of his degradation."
   2. The 1971 Synod document, *Justice in the World*, identified environmental degradation as a sin against the world's poor chiefly caused by consumption in the developed world:
   "Although in general it is difficult to draw a line between what is needed for right use and what is demanded by prophetic witness, we must certainly keep firmly to this principle: our faith demands of us a certain sparing-ness in use, and the church is obliged to live and administer its own goods in such a way that the Gospel is proclaimed to the poor. If instead the church appears to be among the rich and the powerful of this world, its credibility is diminished." —*Justice in the World*, #47

II. Influence of Pope John Paul II
   A. Pope John Paul II was the first to formally address the church's teaching relative to care for creation.
      1. Pope John Paul II provided a reinterpretation of Genesis 1:28, ". . . fill the earth and subdue it," by emphasizing that creation exists to meet human needs, but that it must not be needlessly exploited.
      2. While Pope John Paul II encouraged environmental protection to benefit the human economy, minimal attention was given to the examination of our role as part of "the environment."
   B. 1979's *Redemptor Hominis* expressed concern that humans themselves were being degraded by technology and industrialization.
   C. During the 1984 Synod, Bishop Hamao of Japan emphasized creation in his remarks, noting that work for peace will be effective if we all not only become aware of our deep connection with nature, but also seek harmony with it and admire in it the beauty, wisdom, and love

of the creator. Thus we will be freed of our frenzy for possessions and domination and will become artisans for peace.

D. *Sollicitudo Rei Socialis*, 1987, included a relationship with nature as part of human's *authentic moral development.*

E. 1990 World Day of Peace Message, *The Ecological Crisis: A Common Responsibility*, for the first time:
   1. warned that consumerism is a root cause of environmental degradation, and
   2. broadened the pro-life agenda of the church in stating "respect for life and for the dignity of the human person extends also to the rest of creation."

III. The U.S. bishops respond to growing environmental awareness
   A. History
      1. Pope John Paul II's 1990 World Day of Peace message, *The Ecological Crisis: A Common Responsibility*, set the groundwork for the U.S. bishops' initiatives in this area.
      2. The scientific community for religious leaders invited the U.S. bishops to examine the moral responsibility to environmental problems.
      3. In 1991 the U.S. bishops responded with the pastoral letter *Renewing the Earth*, which challenges the faithful to live in communion with the earth as part of our baptismal call.
      4. In 1992, the National Religious Partnership was formed consisting of the U.S. Catholic Conference, the Coalition on the Environment and Jewish Life, the National Council of Churches of Christ, and the Evangelical Environmental Network.
      5. In 1993, the U.S. bishops formed the Environmental Justice Program, which seeks "to educate and motivate Catholics to a deeper respect for God's creation, and to engage parishes in activities aimed at dealing with environmental problems, particularly as they affect the poor."
      6. In 2001, the U.S. bishops published *Global Climate Change—a plea for dialogue, prudence, and the respect for common good.*

B. "The Biblical Vision of God's Good Earth," as identified by the bishops
  1. "God saw everything that he had made, and indeed, it was very good" (Gn 1:31).
  2. God's people invited all creation to join in their praise of God. "Let the earth bless the Lord; mountains and hills; everything growing from the earth; springs, seas and rivers; water creatures, birds and beasts; bless the Lord; praise and exalt Him above all forever" (adapted from Dn 3:74–81).
  3. Earth is a gift to all creatures, and humans have a special responsibility to "till it and keep it" (Gn 2:15).
  4. Humans are responsible for ensuring that all nature can continue to flourish as God intended. Human sin results in the suffering of all creation, as in the story of the flood. God formed the covenant, however, *with all creation.*
  5. The Sabbath included rest not only for humans, but for the beasts of the field as well. Additionally, every seventh year (a sabbatical year), the earth was to remain fallow (not planted; allowed to rest and be replenished).
  6. Jesus' parables often used the natural world, revealing that *care* is central to the relationship between humans and creation.
C. Several principles were identified in *Global Climate Change* which integrate Care for God's Creation with established social concerns.
  1. A *consistent respect for human life*, which extends to respect for all creation
     a) "Our tradition calls us to protect the life and dignity of the human person, and it is increasingly clear that this task can not be separated from the care and defense of all creation." The ancient call to be *co-creators* is echoed for a new world.
     b) All species, landscapes, and ecosystems give glory to God and are "very good."
     c) "It is appropriate that we treat other creatures and the natural world not just as means to human fulfillment but also as God's creatures, possessing an independent value, worthy of our respect and care."

2. A *God-centered and sacramental view of the universe*, which grounds human accountability for the fate of the earth
   a) Nature itself is revelatory; humans can discern the presence of God in the diversity of creation, the power of tides and storms, the longevity of mountains.
   b) "The whole universe together participates in the divine goodness more perfectly, and represents it better than any single creature whatsoever" (St. Thomas, *Summa Theologica*, Question 48).
   c) Creation has value in and of itself apart from human use.
   d) Stewardship implies that we must care for creation according to God's standards, not ours, and that we must be resourceful in our task of helping the earth flourish.
3. An *option for the poor*, which gives passion to the quest for an equitable and sustainable world
   a) "The goods of the Earth, which in the divine plan should be a common patrimony, often risk becoming the monopoly of a few who often spoil it and, sometimes, destroy it, thereby creating a loss for all humanity" (Pope John Paul II, as quoted in "Communities of Salt and Light").
   b) God has given the fruit of the earth to sustain the entire human family without excluding or favoring anyone.
   c) The poor suffer most directly from environmental decline (e.g., Bhopal, Chernobyl, Love Canal, etc.).
   d) Third world countries and cities in the first world are unable to meet the basic needs of the people.
4. A conception of *authentic development*, which offers a direction for progress that respects human dignity and the limits of material growth.
   a) Unrestrained material growth is not accepted by the church as a model for development.
   b) Moderation is required in the use of earth's goods.
   c) Technology must benefit people and not degrade the earth.
   d) Attention must be given to maintaining the rights of workers *and* environmental protection.

5. An *ethic of solidarity* which affirms the ethical significance of *global interdependence and the common good*
   a) Everyone is affected and everyone is responsible, although those most responsible are often the least affected.
   b) This requires sacrifices of our own self-interest for the good of others and of the earth.
   c) Governments bear a particular burden to protect and preserve creation—the planetary common good—that cannot be protected nor preserved by market forces alone.

INTRODUCTION TO THE ECOLOGICAL IMPACT[4]

Goal: develop a greater appreciation for how our lifestyle choices impact the earth and our global neighbors

I. Ecological Footprinting
   A. Ecological footprinting estimates the "load" imposed on nature by people in terms of the ecosystem area they use.
      1. The ecological footprint of a specified population is the total area of land and water ecosystems required to produce the resources consumed, and to assimilate the wastes produced by that population.
         a) Ecologically productive land is scarce. If all such land were equally divided among the world's population (1996), each person's share would be about 3.7 acres.
         b) Average North Americans currently use three to four times this area.
         c) Reflection question: Who is going without?
      2. The total eco-footprint of humanity may already be thirty percent larger than the sustainable productive capacity of the ecosphere. This means that much of the current growth is based on natural capital depletion, yet billions of people do not yet enjoy even their fair share of natural income.
      3. Economic sustainability depends on achieving both ecological balance and greater social equity.
   B. What is your ecological footprint? What level of impact are you leaving?

1. Includes not only the house in which we live but the forested land used to build it
2. Includes land unearthed to get oil for heating and cooling
3. Includes the land used to produce the food we eat
4. Basically, includes the land needed to sustain our lifestyle and cultural effects
5. In addition, waste that the earth cannot process quickly or easily (trash accumulating in landfills, chemicals in the ground and surface water) becomes a burden for everyone.
6. We are part of nature. The earth meets our material needs, our activities impact the health of the earth, and we rely on the earth for our sustenance.

C. Complete the following Ecological Footprint Assessment:

Home

1. How many people live in your household?
   a) 1 (30 points)
   b) 2 (25 points)
   c) 3 (20 points)
   d) 4 (15 points)
   e) 5 (10 points)

   My points _____

2. How is your home heated?
   a) Natural gas (30 points)
   b) Electricity from coal (40 points)
   c) Oil (50 points)
   d) Electricity from solar, wind, hydroelectric (0 points)

   My points _____

3. How many individual faucets (taps in your kitchen, bathrooms, laundry room, and outside), toilets, and showerheads do you have in your home?
   a) Less than 3 (5 points)
   b) 3–5 (10 points)
   c) 6–8 (15 points)
   d) 9–12 (20 points)
   e) More than 12 (25 points)

My points _____
My Total **Home** points _____

Food

1. How many of your meals per week include meat or fish?
   a) 0 (0 points)
   b) 1–3 (10 points)
   c) 4–6 (15 points)
   d) 7–10 (20 points)
   e) More than 10 (25 points)

My points _____

2. How many homemade meals do you eat per week (including packed lunches)?
   a) Fewer than 10 (25 points)
   b) 10–14 (20 points)
   c) 15–18 (15 points)
   d) More than 18 (10 points)

My points _____

3. When purchasing food items, do you try to buy locally produced goods?
   a) Most of the time (25 points)
   b) Sometimes (50 points)
   c) Rarely (100 points)
   d) Never (125 points)   **My points** _____
My Total **Food** points _____

Transportation

1. What types of vehicles do you and your family own? (add points for **each** vehicle)
   a) Motorcycle (15 points)
   b) Compact (35 points)
   c) Mid-sized (60 points)
   d) Full-sized (75 points)
   e) Sports utility, full-sized van, or truck (100 points)

   My points _____

2. How do you typically get to work, to the store, to school, etc.?
   a) Car (50 points)
   b) Public transportation (25 points)
   c) Car pool (30 points)
   d) Walk (0 points)
   e) Bike, rollerblade, etc. (0 points)

   My points _____

3. If you vacationed last year, where did you go? (add points for **each** vacation)
   a) Vacationed at home or in town (0 points)
   b) Within the state or surrounding states (within a 120 mile radius of home) (5 points)
   c) Between 120 to 500 miles from home (15 points)
   d) Within North American but over 500 miles from home (25 points)
   e) Outside North America (30 points)

   My points _____

4. How many summer weekend trips do you take by car?
   a) 0 (0 points)
   b) 1–3 (10 points)
   c) 4–6 (20 points)
   d) 7–9 (30 points)
   e) 10 or more (40 points)

   My points _____
   My Total **Transportation** points _____

Purchases

1. How many large purchases (stereo, TV, VCR, computer, car, major appliance) has your household made in the past year?
    a)   0 (0 points)
    b)   1–3 (15 points)
    c)   4–6 (30 points)
    d)   More than 6 (45 points)

    My points _____

2. Does your household consciously try to buy energy-efficient products (e.g., compact fluorescent light bulbs, low-flow faucets or toilets, Energy Star computers, appliances with a high efficiency rating, cars with better-than-average gas mileage)?
    a)   Always (0 points)
    b)   Sometimes (20 points)
    c)   Rarely (40 points)
    d)   Never (60 points)

    My points _____
    My Total **Purchases** points _____

Waste

1. Does your household consciously try to reduce the amount of waste and pollution created in the house (through reducing purchases, recycling, reusing, composting, using non-toxic products, etc.)?
    a)   Always (0 points)
    b)   Sometimes (20 points)
    c)   Rarely (40 points)
    d)   Never (60 points)

    My points _____

2. How many garbage bags of waste do you dispose of each week?
    a)   0 (0 points)
    b)   One half-full (5 points)
    c)   1 full (10 points)
    d)   2 full (20 points)
    e)   More than 2 full (30 points)

My points _____
My total **Waste** points _____
My total **Points** from all sections _____

Your Score	Your Ecological Footprint, in Acres
Less than 150	Less than 10
150–350	10–11
355–550	12–13
555–750	14–15
More than 750	More than 16

   D. Personal Reflection:
       1. Compare your Ecological Footprint to:
           a) Each person's global "fair earth share" of 3.7 acres
           b) The U.S. average of about 13 acres
           c) India's average of 1.2 acres
       2. How do your personal or family choices impact the earth?
       3. What institutions or systems need to be addressed to improve
           your use of resources?
       4. What steps can you take? (Both on a personal level and with
           regard to institutional or systemic changes?)

SKILL DEVELOPMENT: TEAM BUILDING
   Goal: identify key aspects of effective team building; participate in team building activities
I. Large Group Discussion
    A. Definition: "a number of persons associated together in work or
        activity."

B. Jesus' use of team: the apostles, disciples, church
C. Catholic social teaching: how we organize our society directly affects human dignity and the capacity of individuals to grow in community
D. The concept of "team" relates directly to our call to build community and to pursue the common good.

II. Characteristics of an Effective Team
A. Shared/common goals
B. Interdependence of team members
C. Specified roles
D. Established norms or rules of behavior
E. Effective communication
F. Mutual accountability

III. Stages of Team Development

Stage	Major Processes	Characteristics
1. Forming (orientation)	Exchange of information; increased interdependency, task exploration; identification of commonalities	Tentative interactions; polite discourse; concern over ambiguity; self-discourse
2. Storming (conflict)	Disagreement over procedures; expression of dissatisfaction; emotional responses; resistance	Criticism of ideas; poor attendance; hostility; polarization and coalition forming
3. Norming (cohesion)	Growth of cohesiveness and unity; establishment of role standards and relationships	Agreement on procedures; reduction in roll ambiguity; increased "we-feeling"
4. Performing	Goal achievement; decision-making; problem (performance) high task orientation; solving	Mutual cooperation; emphasis on performance and production
5. Adjourning	Termination of roles; disintegration and (dissolution) completion of tasks	Withdrawal; increased reduction of dependency independence and emotionality; regret

IV. Characteristics of an Effective Team Member
   A. Works for consensus on decisions
   B. Shares openly and authentically with others regarding personal feelings, opinions, thoughts, and perceptions about team problems and conditions
   C. Involves others in the decision-making process
   D. Trusts, supports, and has genuine concern for other team members
   E. "Owns" problems rather than blaming them on others
   F. When listening, attempts to hear and interpret communication from the other's point of view
   G. Influences others by involving them in the issue(s)
   H. Encourages the development of other team members
   I. Respects and is tolerant of individual differences
   J. Acknowledges and works through conflict openly
   K. Considers and uses new ideas and suggestions from others
   L. Encourages feedback on own behavior
   M. Understands and is committed to team objectives
   N. Does not engage in win or lose activities with other team members
   O. Has skills in understanding what's going on in the group

V. Exercises
   A. "Re-united"
      1. **Objectives:** Pursue common goal, involve all group members
      2. **Group size:** Any number, the bigger the group, the bigger the challenge
      3. **Materials:** Pen and paper
      4. **Directions:** After groups are formed, instruct them to find 5–10 (depending on the time frame) things they all have in common. Challenge them to think creatively: places they have traveled, TV shows they have watched, favorite or least-favorite foods, etc. Then share the most creative commonalities in the large group.
   B. Human Knot
      1. **Goal:** Problem solving, communication, and teamwork
      2. **Materials:** None
      3. **Group size:** At least five, no more than ten

4. **Directions:** The group forms a circle. Each person holds out their right hand and grasps another hand as if shaking hands. Then everyone extends his or her left hand to grab another left hand. No one should hold both hands of the same person or hands of the people on either side of them. The goal is to then untangle into a single circle without releasing hands.

PREPARATION FOR SESSION 3:

CALL TO FAMILY, COMMUNITY, AND PARTICIPATION

- *Read* one of the following excerpts: Job 14:7, Luke 12:24, John 4:13–14, John 12:24, or 1 Corinthians 12:12.
- *Reflect* on your quiet time in nature (at least fifteen minutes).
- *Write* briefly about your quiet reflection:
  How does our view on the dignity of life impact our view of God's creation?
- *Read* these sections of "Communities of Salt and Light": *Sharing the Message: Preaching and Education* and *Supporting the Salt of the Earth: Family, Work, Citizenship.*
- *Complete* the Care for God's Creation Quadrants.

Advocacy

What are we already doing for the theme of *Care for God's Creation* in the area of Advocacy?

1.
2.
3.

What else could we be doing?

1.
2.
3.

Organizing

What are we already doing for the theme of *Care for God's Creation* in the area of Organizing and Development?

1.
2.
3.

What else could we be doing?

1.
2.
3.

Care for God's Creation

Charity

What are we already doing for the theme of *Care for God's Creation* in the area of Charity and Outreach?

1.
2.
3.

What else could we be doing?

1.
2.
3.

Solidarity

What are we already doing for the theme of *Care for God's Creation* in the area of Solidarity and Community Building?

1.
2.
3.

What else could we be doing?

1.
2.
3.

SESSION 2 RESOURCES

From the United States Conference of Catholic Bishops

     800-235-8722

     www.usccb.org

     St. Francis Prayer Card

          Featuring the "Canticle of the Sun"—written by St. Francis of Assisi—this newly redesigned, folded prayer card displays a beautiful iconic image of St. Francis on the front panel.

          No. 5-024

     "Global Climate Change"

          A Plea for Dialogue, Prudence, and the Common Good

          English: No. 5-431, 28 pp.

          Spanish: No. 5-855, 32 pp.

          And God Saw That It Was Good: Catholic Theology and the Environment

          Edited by Drew Christiansen, SJ, and Walter Grazer.

          No. 5-089, 348 pp.

     "Let the Earth Bless the Lord: God's Creation and Our Responsibility"

          A Catholic Approach to the Environment

          No. 5-085, 44 pp.

          "Peace with God the Creator, Peace with All Creation"

          No. 032-X, 53 pp.

          "Renewing the Face of the Earth"

          No. 766-9, 80 pp.

          "Renewing the Earth: An Invitation to Reflection and Action on Environment in Light of Catholic Social Teaching

          No. 468-6, 20 pp.

          "The Ecological Crisis"

          A Common Responsibility

          No. 332-9, 14 pp.

          "Hope for a Renewed Earth" (video)

          No. 5-072, 60 minutes

          "The Earth Is the Lord's" (video)

          No. 058-3, 13 minutes

SESSION 3:

CALL TO FAMILY, COMMUNITY, AND PARTICIPATION

AGENDA
- Prayer: "Call to Family"
- Recap/Overview
  - Assignments
    - How did your recent quiet time with nature differ from your previous time?
    - What insights have you gained regarding the dignity of *all* life?
  - Recap
    - Last session introduced our role as caretakers for all of God's creation,
    - Provided a means of assessing our own impact on creation,
    - Explored team building and development.
  - Overview
    - This session will broaden our realm of God-centered relationships from the personal to the interpersonal.
- Catholic Social Teaching: Call to Family, Community, and Participation
- Break
- Skill Development: Brainstorming
- Preparation for Session 4: Option for the Poor and Vulnerable
- Evaluation
- Closing Prayer

CALL TO FAMILY

Quiet Gathering

Opening Prayer: Lord Jesus, you have told us that wherever two or more are gathered in your name, you are in our midst. Help us to trust in your presence today as we gather to praise you, to discern your will for us, and to put it into action at home, in our church, and in our world. We thank and praise you forever and ever. Amen.

Scripture Reading: Matthew 12:46–50
Shared Reflection: What does the word "family" mean to you? Who is part of your family? What do you learn in family that is important to community?
Litany for God's People

Response: Lord, with your grace, help us to be people of conscience, compassion, and action.

#1 *We pray for families.* For the love cultivated and for the understanding of human dignity, may our families grow in the love of God to truly be domestic church. We pray:
Response

#2 *We pray for families.* For the laughter shared and tears shed; for the experience of community; may our families grow in the love of God to truly be domestic church. We pray:
Response

#3 *We pray for families.* For the development of values and the model of just action, may our families grow in the love of God to truly be domestic church. We pray:
Response

#4 *We pray for community.* We pray for friends and colleagues, past and present; may we seize the opportunity to work together to protect the life, dignity, and rights of the person. We pray:
Response

#5 *We pray for community.* We pray for friends and colleagues, for their support and challenge; may we seize the opportunity to promote the well-being of our families and communities. We pray:
Response

#6 *We pray for community.* We pray for friends and colleagues, for their faith and vision; may we seize the opportunity to pursue the common good. We pray:
Response

#7 We pray for the poor and oppressed. For the rejection experienced daily, may we recognize what is truly holy by acknowledging the divine presence in our brothers and sisters. We pray:
Response

#8 We pray for the poor and oppressed. For the powerlessness experienced daily, may we recognize what is truly holy by honoring the sacred covenant between God and the poor. We pray:
Response

#9 We pray for the poor and oppressed. For the isolation experienced daily, may we recognize what is truly holy by acting justly, loving tenderly, and walking humbly with God. We pray:
Response

Personal Intentions

Leader: "Gathering our prayers and our praise into one, we offer the prayer that Jesus taught us."

The Lord's Prayer

Closing Song

CATHOLIC SOCIAL TEACHING:
CALL TO FAMILY, COMMUNITY, AND PARTICIPATION

Goal: develop an understanding of how the social mission is passed on, how we participate in the mission on different levels, and how that mission may be applied at the parish level.

I.   Sharing the Message: Preaching and Education (from "Communities of Salt and Light")

    A.   Action for justice is integral to the gospel message: "Our social doctrine is an integral part of our faith; we need to pass it on clearly, creatively, and consistently."[5]

        1.   Preaching

            a)   In 1971, a synod of bishops in Rome issued a statement called "Justice in the World," which stated: "Action on behalf of justice and participation in the transformation of the world fully appear to us as a constitutive dimension of the preaching of the gospel."

                (1)   Constitutive elements of the Catholic faith:

                    (a)   Scripture

                    (b)   Sacrament

                    (c)   Social

            b)   The U.S. bishops' statement, "Communities of Salt and Light" echoes this notion: "Preaching that ignores the social dimensions of our faith does not truly reflect the gospel of Jesus Christ."[6]

        2.   Education

            a)   "Communities of Salt and Light" further challenges the parish: "Our social doctrine must also be an essential part of the curriculum and life of our schools, religious education programs, sacramental preparation and Christian initiation activities. . . . Every parish should regularly assess how well our social teaching is shared in its formation and educational ministries."[7]

    B.   Small Group

        1.   Reflect on and then complete the "Is the Preaching and Teaching About Justice Too Salty, Too Light, or Just Right?" questionnaire.

2. Briefly share your responses to the questionnaire in small groups.

3. Discuss how we, in our parish, participate in and encourage the teaching of the social dimension of the gospel.

IS THE PREACHING AND TEACHING ABOUT JUSTICE TOO SALTY, TOO LIGHT, OR JUST RIGHT?

Please circle, fill-in, check, or indicate your answers to the following questions.

1. In the past month, how often have you noted "justice," "mercy," "fidelity," and/or "truth," in a homily or in personal prayer?

   Always   Often   Sometimes   Rarely   Never

2. Are issues such as poverty, race, overconsumption, the environment, labor, healthcare, ethnic conflicts, and others discussed

   a. from the pulpit as they pertain to the gospel?

   Always   Often   Sometimes   Rarely   Never

   b. in parish committees?

   Always   Often   Sometimes   Rarely   Never

   c. in youth or adult formation programs?

   Always   Often   Sometimes   Rarely   Never

3. Are you sent forth from liturgy to actively live out the gospel in your family, community, and with "the least among us"?

   Always   Often   Sometimes   Rarely   Never

4. Does your parish have a social ministry committee? Is it in relationship with the diocesan Parish Social Ministry office?

   Yes   No

5. Is your parish in relationship with a Catholic Campaign for Human Development funded group?

   Yes   No

6. Is your parish in relationship with a parish or diocese in another country or culture?

   Yes   No

7. Does your parish participate in Operation Rice Bowl?

   Yes   No

8. Does your parish have or participate in a legislative advocacy network?
   Yes   No

9. Does your parish participate in Bread for the World's Offering of Letters?
   Yes   No

10. Does your parish participate in local or global crisis alleviation efforts?
    Yes   No

FAMILY, WORK, AND CITIZENSHIP

I. Catholic social teaching principle: Call to Family, Community, and Participation
   A. Addresses God's invitation to know and love God through meaningful and compassionate relationships with *all* of God's creation, as well as with the structures and systems that support them
       1. Our understanding of God and God's creation can be viewed on three levels:
           a) **Personal**: Me and God; God and me
           b) **Interpersonal**: Me, my family, my community
           c) **Structural**: The systems that facilitate the manner in which societies function (political, economic, cultural, social).
       2. Our relationship with God is deepened as we work toward fidelity to the demands of the relationship on all three levels.
   B. The first level of reality involves the individual.
       1. The very core of creation: each person is made in the image and likeness of God.
           a) Each and every person is sacred and loved and holds a special relationship with God.
           b) "I have called you by name, you are mine. . . . You are precious in my sight" (Is 43:1, 4).
       2. Primary focus of our culture
           a) Rugged individualist
           b) Reinforces singular idea of salvation through personal prayer and reflection—an inward journey
   C. The second level is the interpersonal level—the family and community.

1. Family—our first and primary community
   a) From the moment we are conceived, we are in a relationship with others; our survival (salvation) is intimately connected with others.
   b) As domestic church, the family is called to mirror the love, communication, and solidarity that is expressed in the Trinity.
      1) The very nature of God is relational and is glorified in the Trinity.
      2) Our faith, and hence salvation, is fundamentally social.
2. "The human person is not only sacred, but social. We realize our dignity and rights in relationship with others, in community. . . . The family has major contributions to make in addressing questions of social justice. It is where we learn and act on our values."[8]
   a) Through our relationships with others, our knowledge and vision of, and therefore our relationship to, God is broadened.
      1) In other words, justice is realized in the integrity with which we live out our relationships, be they with family members, neighbors, business contracts, other governments, the poor, etc.
      2) Hence, contrary to our culturally dominant focus on the individual, our faith is profoundly social. Therefore, our salvation is through others.
   b) The essence of justice is "fidelity to the demands of the relationship."[9]
D. The third level involves the structures and systems which facilitate and impact personal, familial, and communal life. (This is the focus Sessions 5, 6, and 7.) We are called not to live in isolation, but to full participation in the human community.
   1. "'The dignity of the human person involves the right to take an active part in public affairs and to contribute one's part to the common good of the citizens.' As Pope Pius XII pointed out, 'The human individual, far from being an object, a merely passive element in the social order, is in fact . . . its subject, its foundation and its end.'"—*Pacem in Terris*, #26

2. ". . . it belongs to the laity, without waiting passively for orders and directives, to take the initiative freely and to infuse a Christian spirit into the mentality, customs, laws and structures of their communities."—*Populorum Progressio*, #81

3. "It is not enough to recall principles, state intentions, point to crying injustices and utter prophetic denunciations; these words will lack real weight unless they are accompanied for each individual by a livelier awareness of personal responsibility and effective action."—*Octogesima Adveniens*, #48

II. Skill Development: Brainstorming

Goal: articulate the role community plays both in deepening one's relationship to God (i.e., faith) and in practicing justice

"Our parishes are clearly called to help people live their faith in the world, helping them to understand and act on the social dimensions of the Gospel in their everyday lives."
—"Communities of Salt and Light"[10]

A. Large Group Work
1. Brainstorming Tactics
    a) Stay focused on the topic—do not stray
    b) Anything goes
    c) Push the ridiculous—be innovative
    d) Respect each others' suggestions
    e) Do not analyze suggestions
    f) Fully utilize the designated time
2. Application: Brainstorm strategies to strengthen the parish community

B. Small Group Work
1. Choose one of the strategies among those listed from the brainstorming session.
2. Brainstorm ways in which a parish can act on that concern.

C. Large Group Discussion of Programs
  1. Small groups share strategies and brainstorming process
  2. Reflection: How do the strategies meet:
      a) The need?
      b) The gospel call?
D. Personal Reflection
  1. What are you willing to do to make this happen?

PREPARATION FOR SESSION 4:

OPTION FOR THE POOR AND VULNERABLE

- *Talk* to an adult or child who is a member of your parish community and ask:
  - What does the parish mean to them?
  - What would they like to see happen in the parish?
  - What are they willing to do to help make it happen?
- *Write* a brief reflection on that which impressed you most significantly from the conversation.
- *Read*
  - This section in "Communities of Salt and Light": *Serving the Least of These: Outreach and Charity*
  - Styles of Ministry (p. 16–18)
- *Complete* the Call to Family, Community, and Participation Quadrants

Advocacy

What are we already doing for the theme of *Family and Community* in the area of Advocacy?

1.
2.
3.

What else could we be doing?

1.
2.
3.

Organizing

What are we already doing for the theme of *Family and Community* in the area of Organizing and Development?

1.
2.
3.

What else could we be doing?

1.
2.
3.

Call to Family, Community, and Participation

Charity

What are we already doing for the theme of *Family and Community* in the area of Charity and Outreach?

1.
2.
3.

What else could we be doing?

1.
2.
3.

Solidarity

What are we already doing for the theme of *Family and Community* in the area of Solidarity and Community Building?

1.
2.
3.

What else could we be doing?

1.
2.
3.

SESSION 3 RESOURCES

PREACHING

Preaching the Just Word is a national program sponsored by the Woodstock Theological Center to assist priests and other ministers of the gospel to be more effective in preaching social justice. Conceived by Walter J. Burghardt, S.J., the project is coordinated by both Father Burghardt and Father Raymond B. Kemp. Visit www.georgetown.edu/centers/woodstock/pjw.htm

The Living Pulpit is a unique source of help to energize sermons by renewing confidence in the power of the preached Word. Visit www.pulpit.org

Liturgy, Justice, and the Reign of God, Frank Henderson, et al. (Paulist Press, 800-836-3161, www.paulistpress.com)

Web sites:

National Catholic Reporter: The Peace Pulpit: Homilies by Bishop Thomas J. Gumbleton www.nationalcatholicreporter.org/peace

Sunday and Weekday Liturgy: Sermons and other Resources www.prayingeachday.org/prayersites.html#sun

EDUCATION

"Sharing Catholic Social Teaching: Challenges and Directions"
800-235-8722
www.usccb.org
English: No. 5-281, 32 pp.
Spanish: No. 5-803, 32 pp.

"Leader's Guide to *Sharing Catholic Social Teaching*"
800-235-8722
www.usccb.org
No. 5-366, 64 pp.

Web sites:

National Catholic Education Association www.ncea.org

Office for Social Justice, Archdiocese of St. Paul and Minneapolis (has a PowerPoint presentation available for download on Catholic social teaching and education) osjspm.org/justed.htm

North American Forum on the Catechumenate www.naforum.org/default.htm

Catholic Relief Services– Programs on Catholic social teaching and global solidarity www.catholicrelief.org/index.cfm

Catholic Campaign for Human Development/Poverty USA (On-line Education Center, Lesson Plans Grades K-12, Adult Education) www.nccbuscc.org/cchd/povertyusa/index.htm

FAMILY

"Follow the Way of Love"
A Pastoral Message of the U.S. Catholic Bishops to Families
www.usccb.org
800-235-8722
English: No. 677-8

"Families: Black and Catholic, Catholic and Black"
Readings, Resources, and Family Activities
www.usccb.org
800-235-8722
No. 890-8, 180 pp.

"Putting Children and Families First"
A Challenge for Our Church, Nation, and World
www.usccb.org
800-235-8722
No. 469-4, 24 pp.

"A Catholic Campaign for Children and Families"
Parish Resource Manual
www.usccb.org
800-235-8722
No. 525-9, 88 pp.

SKILL AREA: BRAINSTORMING

Brain Storm: Tap into Your Creativity to Generate Awesome Ideas and Remarkable Results, Jason R. Rich (Career Press, 2003).

Brainstorming: The Book of Topics, Marty Fligor (Creative Learning Press, 1990).

The Busy Exec.com/Tips on Brainstorming
www.thebusyexec.com/pro_development/s_cp_b.htm

OPTION FOR THE POOR AND VULNERABLE

AGENDA
- Prayer: "Blessed are the Poor"
- Recap/Overview
  - What did you learn from your conversations with the child or adult from your parish?
  - What have we learned together thus far?
  - Are we meeting our expectations?
- Catholic Social Teaching: Option for the Poor and Vulnerable
  "No one is justified in keeping for his exclusive use what he does not need when others lack necessities."—*Populorum Progressio*, Pope Paul VI
- Skit and Discussion: "Where You Stand Depends on Where You Sit"
- Break
- Skill Development: Program Development
  - Large Group Discussion
  - Small Group Work: Issue Identification and Goal Setting
  - Large Group Summary
- Preparation for Session 5: Rights and Responsibilities
- Evaluation
- Closing Prayer

"Blessed are the Poor"

Call to Worship

Song: "The Lord Hears the Cry of the Poor"

Opening Prayer

Meditation[11]
Some excerpts from Pope Paul's encyclical *Populorum Progressio.*

1. Introduction
Progress means many things to the peoples of the world. For some it means escape from hunger, from poverty, from disease and ignorance. For others it means sharing out more fully the good things of civilization.

2. Pope John, and the council he inspired, taught us to hear the whole world's cry for help: the hungry crying for good to those who have too much, the people crying in pain to the people whose duty is love.

3. Progress can mean seeing more clearly what makes life really human. Or it can mean a whole people setting off courageously to find their self-fulfillment.

4. All this human development the church is watching closely. The church hears all with grief, and commands each one of us to listen, and to act.

5. The facts
What progress do people want to make? They want freedom from the depths of poverty. They want security, enough to eat, good health, a steady job, more say in how their lives are run and not so much oppression. They want to be treated like human beings. They want the chance of better education.

6. In a word, what they want is more. They want more to do. They want to know more, and have more, because what they really want is to be more.

7. Yet all the time they go on wanting more, for most of them things are getting worse not better.

8. The church and progress
The church is taught by Christ. He preached his gospel to the poor. He said this was a sign that he was sent by God. The church herself has always been committed to human progress as well as to the gospel. . . .

9. The time has come for more than local, isolated action. All people must act together, to tackle every side of this problem of human progress, the great social problem of today.

10. As an expert on humankind, the church has much to offer. Like Christ, she lives to witness the truth. She was founded to set up the Kingdom of Heaven right down here on earth. She was not founded to dominate the earth. Yet here she is, among people now, reading the signs of the times. These signs of life she then explains for all in the gospel's light.

11. To become what we can become
In God's plan, every single person is called upon to grow. From birth, all of us carry within ourselves the seeds of personal growth. All of us can bear fruit proposed for us by God. This is progress.

12. God gives to every person both intellect and will. So everyone is responsible for growing, as they should. Those who teach people and those who surround them in life can help, as they can hinder. . . .

13. From what is less to what is more genuinely human

What is less human? The material poverty of people who lack the means of life; the moral poverty of people crippled by selfishness; the network of oppression fostered by the abuse of power; exploitation of the workers; and crooked business deals.

14. What is more human?

The end of want, everyone having enough; the end of social ills of every kind; more knowledge; more culture; respect for the dignity of others; the spirit of poverty; co-operation for the common good; the will for peace.

15. What can we do?

"Fill the earth and conquer it." The Bible makes it clear that people, by their work and by their wits, should give new meaning to all creation. All things were made for people. People have the right to find in the world around them all they need for life and for progress. God has made the earth and all it contains for all people to share.

16. "If any man is rich but shuts his eyes to one who stands in need, the love of God is missing from his heart." (1 John)

17. "If any man is rich and does give help to one who stands in need, he only gives the poor man what was already his. The earth was made for all, not just for the rich." (St. Ambrose)

18. Priorities

The present situation demands great courage as we fight against injustice. It calls for radical reform without delay. All of us might play our part, according to our gifts, and give of our possessions for the Gospel is a ferment, exciting in the human heart a fierce regard for human dignity.

19. The first thing a country should develop is basic education. Starving a person's mind hurts them as much as starving their body. Literacy is the foundation stone of self-confidence and progress. People who are literate can act for themselves.

20. National planning is needed to encourage and to stimulate, coordinate, support and integrate the efforts being made by individuals and teams of people below the level of the state. Planning is needed to banish the inequality, to fight discrimination, to set people free and give them full responsibility for their own bodily well being for their own moral and spiritual progress.

21. Family life is the bedrock of human society. A deeper humanism is what the world most needs, a humanism that is complete and seeks the full development of the whole personality in every person.

22. Final appeal

All Catholics are called to act. The Bishops lay down principles. The laity must act using their own initiative, not waiting for instructions.

23. Christians of every kind can work together to build a better world, a world made human by the end of selfishness and by the reign of love.

24. All people of good will must know how peace comes from development. All those who hear the cries of human suffering, all those who work to set the world aright, are true apostles. The daily bread they bring to others is a sign of more than human love. It is a sign of Providence.

25. If development is now the name for peace, who can refuse such work? We plead in anguish and in the name of Christ.

Shared Reflection: After a few minutes of silent reflection, all are invited to share their reflections on the meditation.

Closing Prayer: Lord, God, you hear the cries of the poor. Help us to open our ears to hear those same cries and to work together to build a better, more human world. We ask this is your son's name, who lives with us for ever and ever. Amen.

CATHOLIC SOCIAL TEACHING:
OPTION FOR THE POOR AND VULNERABLE[12]

Goal: develop an understanding of the roots, meaning, and implications of the church's preferential option for the poor.

I. Sociological Clarification
   A. Identify: Who are the poor?
      1. Those who are economically disadvantaged and materially deprived, who as a result experience powerlessness and oppression
      2. "Option" as a verb; not an exclusive option, but preferential
   B. Assume a new perspective
      1. Optic Model: Look at and assess the world through a new lens, that of the poor.
      2. Parent Model: Knowing that we are children of God, look at and assess the world through the eyes of a parent whose children suffer.

II. Theological Foundation
   A. Why an option for the poor?
      1. Rooted in scripture and tradition: Spirituality toward poor from the time of the prophets
         a) "This, rather, is the fasting that I wish: releasing those bound unjustly, untying the thongs of the yoke; setting free the oppressed, breaking every yoke; sharing your bread with the hungry, sheltering the oppressed and the homeless; clothing the naked when you see them, and not turning your back on your own" (Is 58:6–7 *NAB*).
         b) "Thus says the LORD: Do what is right and just. Rescue the victim from the hand of his oppressor. Do not wrong or oppress the resident alien, the orphan, or the widow, and do not shed innocent blood in this place" (Jer 22:3–4 *NAB*).
      2. Christians make an option for the poor because Jesus did.
         a) "The spirit of the Lord is upon me, because he has anointed me to bring good news to the poor. He has sent me to proclaim release to the captives, and recovery of sight to the blind, to let the oppressed go free, to proclaim a year of the Lord's favor" (Lk 4:18–19).

b) Jesus' mission echoes the call of the prophets.
3. The Christian community evangelizes the poor *and* the poor evangelize the Christian community.
   a) In the first letter of John, we read: "How does God's love abide in anyone who has the world's goods and sees a brother or sister in need and yet refuses to help?" (1 Jn 3:17).
   b) St. Ambrose, one of the Fathers of the Church, said:

"You are not making a gift of your possessions to the poor person. You are handing over to him what is his. For what had been given in common for the use of all, you have arrogated to yourself. The world is given to all, and not only to the rich."

B. Modern Catholic social teaching strengthens the call
1. Second Vatican Council included theme in the Constitution on the Church in the Modern World (*Gaudium et Spes*) in 1965:

"The joys and the hopes, the griefs and the anxieties of the people of this age, especially those who are poor or in any way afflicted, these too are the joys and hopes, the grief and anxieties of the followers of Christ." (#1)

2. Pope Paul VI echoed the theme when he spoke to the United Nations in 1965:

"We make our own the voice of the poor, the disinherited, the suffering, of those who hunger and thirst for justice, for the dignity of life, for freedom, for well-being and progress." (#11)

3. Pope Paul VI wrote in *Populorum Progressio*: "No one is justified in keeping for his exclusive use what he does not need when others lack necessities." (#23)
4. The Latin American bishops' meeting at Medellin in 1968 said: "The Church—the people of God—will lend its support to the downtrodden of every social class so that they might come to know their rights and how to make use of them." (#20)
5. In 1971, the Synod of bishops, in *Justice in the World*, said: ". . . the Church is obliged to live and administer its own goods in such a

way that the Gospel is proclaimed to the poor. If instead, the Church appears to be among the rich and powerful of this world, its credibility is diminished." (#47)

6. The U.S. bishops, in their 1986 Pastoral on "Economic Justice for All: Pastoral Letter on Catholic Social Teaching and the U.S. Economy" said: "As followers of Christ, we are challenged to make a fundamental 'option for the poor'—to speak for the voiceless, to defend the defenseless, to assess lifestyles, policies and social institutions in terms of their impact on the poor . . . those with the greatest needs require the greatest response."

7. The U.S. bishops, in their 1993 statement, "Communities of Salt and Light," echo the call to parish communities: "Our parishes should be measured by our help for the hungry, the homeless, the troubled and the alienated—in our community and beyond. . . . Catholic teaching calls us to serve those in need and to change the structures which deny people their dignity and rights as children of God. Service and action, charity and justice are complementary components of parish social ministry." (III, C)

8. In his Apostolic Letters at the close of the Great Jubilee of the Year 2000, *Novo Millennio Ineunte*, Pope John Paul II states: "Certainly we need to remember that no one can be excluded from our love, since 'through his Incarnation the Son of God has united himself in some fashion with every person.' Yet, as the unequivocal words of the Gospel reminds us, there is a special presence of Christ in the poor, and this required the Church to make a preferential option for them. This option is a testimony to the nature of God's love, to his providence and mercy; and in some way history is still filled with the seeds of the Kingdom of God which Jesus himself sowed during his earthly life whenever he responded to those who came to him with their spiritual and material needs."

III. Pastoral Applications: What can you do for the poor?
   A. Do *not* live in ways that oppress the poor.
   B. *Do* live in ways that break the cycle of oppression.

1. Affective: let the poor touch your heart.
2. Effective (direct): work/live directly with the poor.
3. Effective (indirect): live life so that all actions are part of transforming society towards greater justice for those who are poor.
   C. Summary
1. A few live *like* the poor.
2. Some live *with* the poor.
3. All live *for* the poor.

IV. Personal Implications: How can I live out the option for the poor?
   A. Acknowledge your own vulnerability.
   B. Adopt a simpler lifestyle.
   C. Involve yourself in parish or community ministries; "tithe your time."
   D. Make friends with people who are poor.

V. Large Group Question (brainstorming):
   A. What are you (personally and/or your parish) doing to exercise the "option for the poor?"
   B. List and connect those actions with the Styles of Ministry Quadrants.

SKILL DEVELOPMENT: PROGRAM DEVELOPMENT[13]

Goal: (1) develop a consistent and logical method of identifying clear-cut issues and developing strategies to address those issues; (2) refine brainstorming skills

I. Large Group Presentation: Program Development
   A. These are seven (7) steps of Program Development:
1. Diagnosis
2. Define Goal
3. Brainstorm Strategies
4. Analysis
5. Decision-making
6. Implementation
7. Evaluation
      Note: Diagnosis, Define Goal, and Brainstorm Strategies will be discussed in this session. The remaining steps will be addressed in Session 5.

B. Diagnosis: Break problems down into "winnable" issues
    1. "Winnable"
        a) Has the potential for being solved, i.e., "won"
        b) Has clearly defined and manageable parameters
        c) Addresses: Who? What? Where?
    2. Problem → Issue: Poverty → 13 percent of the parish children go to school hungry every day
        a) Who: school-aged children
        b) What: hungry from not eating breakfast
        c) Where: parish
    3. Where you stand depends on where you sit: Perspective is important
        a) Who is naming the problem, identifying the issue?
            (1) Which side of the issue are *you* on: the giver or the receiver?
            (2) If the giver, how do you know what the receivers (participants) want or need?
        b) **Essential**: good planning must actively and adequately involve target population in the planning, implementation process: **No Tokenism**
            (1) Recruit those for whom the program is designed to help in the decision-making process, *or*
            (2) Begin with where you are and your needs:
                (a) I am retired and want to be involved
                (b) I am looking for a job and need moral support
C. Define Goal
    1. Addresses what you hope to achieve in a given time frame
        a) Can be the positive corollary to the stated issue
        b) **Answers**: Who, What, Where *and* When
    2. Example: The parish children who go to school hungry will receive breakfast during the school year.
D. Brainstorm Strategies
    1. A viable strategy is any possible way to achieve your goal.
        a) Strategies for social programs will generally fall under one of the four styles of community work: charity, advocacy, organizing, or solidarity.

        b) Examples: School breakfast program; soup kitchen; advocate for better government subsidies; organize a food co-op, etc.

    2. Be careful not to confuse necessary steps to implement a strategy with the strategies themselves.

        a) For example, bulletin announcements will help spread the word about a breakfast program; but announcements alone will not feed the children.

        b) Do *not* confuse strategy with steps of implementation

    3. Brainstorm: The sky is the limit here; no holds barred

        a) There is no analysis or discussion at this stage

        b) Let the creative juices flow

E. Analysis

    1. Look at each program and assess its feasibility.

        a) What are the advantages and disadvantages of each idea?

        b) How much time, money, resources, people, energy, etc. will be needed for each idea?

        c) What are the criteria for choosing?

        d) Who needs to be involved in the decision? Who has final say? Where are they likely to stand?

    2. How are those for whom the program is designed involved in the planning, decision-making, implementation, etc.?

F. Decision-Making

    1. Which idea/plan is accepted? (there may be several)

    2. Who needs to be informed, consulted, etc.?

G. Implementation

    1. Who is willing to oversee the plan?

    2. What needs to be done?

    3. Who will do what, where, and how?

    4. How will you hold each other accountable?

H. Evaluation

    1. At what point do we need to evaluate?

    2. Who should be involved?

    3. How will it be done?

    4. What are the measures?

II. Small Group Work: The problem will be given to you; as a group you are to walk through steps A, B, and C. Identify an issue and define your goal; spend most of your time brainstorming strategies to meet your goal.

III. Large Group Feedback Session

Preparation for Session 5:

Rights and Responsibilities

- *Talk* with someone from the target population for whom you hope to minister or to whom you are already ministering to get their perspective.
  - Introduce yourself and state the common denominator (e.g., "I've seen you at the 9:00 Mass," etc.)
  - Share some information about each other
  - Suggest your own concern about society and ask about his or her concerns.
- *Write* a brief reflection on what you learned from your conversation:
  - How were his or her concerns similar or different from your own?
  - Were your assumptions about this person challenged? How?
- *Read*
  - From "Communities of Salt and Light": *Rights and Responsibilities: Legislative Action*
  - The Bill of Rights, p. 159
  - U.N. Universal Declaration of Human Rights, p. 160
  - *Pacem in Terris*, Rights and Responsibilities, p. 165
- *Complete* the Option for the Poor and Vulnerable Quadrants, p.72.

Advocacy

What are we already doing for the theme of *Option for the Poor and Vulnerable* in the area of Advocacy?
1.
2.
3.

What else could we be doing?
1.
2.
3.

Organizing

What are we already doing for the theme of *Option for the Poor and Vulnerable* in the area of Organizing and Development?
1.
2.
3.

What else could we be doing?
1.
2.
3.

Option for the Poor and Vulnerable

Charity

What are we already doing for the theme of *Option for the Poor and Vulnerable* in the area of Charity and Outreach?
1.
2.
3.

What else could we be doing?
1.
2.
3.

Solidarity

What are we already doing for the theme of *Option for the Poor and Vulnerable* in the area of Solidarity and Community Building?
1.
2.
3.

What else could we be doing?
1.
2.
3.

Session 4 Resources
Preferential Option for the Poor

Resources from the United States Conference of Catholic Bishops
800-235-8722
www.usccb.org

Catholic Campaign for Human Development: The National Conference of Catholic Bishops (NCCB) established the Catholic Campaign for Human Development, the Catholic Church's domestic anti-poverty program, in 1969 with two purposes. The first purpose was to raise funds to support "organized groups of white and minority poor to develop economic strength and political power." The second purpose was to "educate the People of God to a new knowledge of today's problems . . . that can lead to some new approaches that promote a greater sense of solidarity."

The CCHD philosophy emphasizes empowerment and participation for the poor. By helping the poor to participate in the decisions and actions that affect their lives, CCHD empowers them to move beyond poverty.

CCHD has many resources on the justice education and the church's commitment to the preferential option for and with the poor. Please visit www.usccb.org/cchd/index.htm *and* www.povertyusa.org

"A Place At The Table—Catholic Recommitment to Overcome Poverty and to Respect the Dignity of All God's Children"

The "Barrio Series," a video series produced by the Columban Fathers. Presentation of the Third World option for the poor."(Call 202-529-5115)

Option for the Poor: A Hundred Years of Vatican Social Teaching, Donald Dorr. (Orbis Books, 800-258-5838, www.maryknollmall.org)

"Economic Justice"
Tenth Anniversary Edition of Economic Justice for All
Catholic Social Teaching and the U.S. Economy
English: No. 5-135, 160 pp.

"A Catholic Framework for Economic Life"
English Poster: No. 5-137
Spanish Poster: No. 5-138,
English Card: No. 5-139
Spanish Card: No. 5-140

"A Decade After *Economic Justice for All*"
Continuing Principles, Changing Context, New Challenges
  English: No. 5-040, 16 pp.
  Spanish: No. 5-041, 16 pp.
"For Justice: A Video Magazine" (Videotape)
  Tells the story of *Economic Justice for All* through employment,
  housing, farming issues, and citizen participation.
  No. 5-350, 28 minutes

Skills: Program Development

Parish Social Ministry: Strategies for Success, Tom Ulrich (Ave Maria Press,
  800-282-1865, www.avemariapress.com)
*The Empowerment Process: Centering Social Ministry in the Life of the Local
  Christian Community,* Mary Ellen Durbin, et al (Paulist Press, 800-836-
  3161, www.paulistpress.com)
Go and Do the Same, Nancy Vendouras, C.S.J. (Paulist Press, 800-836-3161,
  www.paulistpress.com)
Tomorrow's Parish: Choosing your Future, Rev. David Baldwin of the Office
  of Research and Planning, Archdiocese of Chicago (312-751-7999, ext
  8345)
Collaborative Ministry: Skills and Guidelines, Loughlan Sofield, S.T. and
  Carroll Juliano, S.H.C.J. (Ave Maria Press, 1-800-282-1865,
  www.avemariapress.com)

SESSION 5:

RIGHTS AND RESPONSIBILITIES

AGENDA
- Prayer: "Going Upstream"
- Recap/Overview
  - What did you learn from your conversations?
  - Today's agenda
- Catholic Social Teaching: Rights and Responsibilities
  - Review the four "rights" documents
  - Introduction to the structures and systems that organize society
- Skill Development: Advocacy
- Break
- Skill Development: Program Development
- Preparation for Session 6: The Dignity of Work and the Rights of Workers
- Evaluation: Oral
- Closing Prayer

"Going Upstream"

Call to Worship

Opening Prayer

A Parable of Good Works[14]

Once upon a time there was a small village on the edge of a river, the people there were good and the life in the village was good. One day a villager noticed a baby floating down the river and swam out to save the baby from drowning.

The next day this same villager was walking along the riverbank and noticed two babies in the river. He called for help, and both babies were rescued from the swift waters. The following day four babies were seen caught in the turbulent current. And then eight, then more, and still more.

The villagers organized themselves quickly, setting up watchtowers and training teams of swimmers who could resist the swift waters and rescue babies. Rescue squads were soon working 24 hours a day. And each day the number of helpless babies floating down the river increased.

The villagers organized themselves efficiently. The rescue squads were now snatching many children each day. Groups were trained to give mouth-to-mouth resuscitation. Others prepared formula and provided clothing for the chilled babies. Many, particularly elderly women, were involved in making clothing and knitting blankets. Still others provided foster homes and placement. While not all the babies could be saved, the villagers felt they were doing well to save as many as they could each day. Indeed, the village priest blessed them in their good work. Life in the village continued on this basis.

One day, however, someone raised the question, "But where are all these babies coming from? Who is throwing them into the river? Why? Let's organize a team to go upstream and see who's doing it."

The seeming logic of the elders countered: *"And if we go upstream who will operate the rescue operations? We need every concerned person here."*

"But don't you see," cried the one lone voice, "if we find out who is throwing them in, we can stop the problem and no babies will drown. By going upstream we can eliminate the cause of the problem."

"It is too risky."

And so the number of babies in the river increases daily. Those saved increase, but those who drown increase even more.

Shared Reflection

The Lord's Prayer

Catholic Social Teaching: Rights and Responsibilities

I. Discussion: Rights Documents

 Goal: *Develop a sense of both the rights and responsibilities of individuals as identified by various secular and religious documents.*

 A. Compare the U.S. Bill of Rights with the U.N. Declaration on Human Rights. What are the major differences/similarities between the two?

 B. Compare the two secular documents with *Pacem in Terris*.

 C. What are the major differences/similarities here?

II. Discussion: Distinctions Among the Nature of Relationships[15]

 Goal: *Use a semantic approach to develop a deeper understanding of the structural nature of social concerns.*

Personal/Interpersonal	Structural
Victim	Cause
Mercy, charity	Justice
Compassion	Peace
Conversion/influence	Power
Attitudes	Organizations
Personal sin	Social sin
Guilt/blame	Responsibility for change
Program	Policy
Autonomy/relationship	Interdependence
Humanities	Social sciences

III. Skill Development: Advocacy

 Goal: *Develop a sense of the What? Why? and How? of advocacy.*

 A. What is advocacy and why is it necessary?

 B. How does it relate to human rights and responsibilities?

 C. How do we do it?

 See The Vision of a Parish's Social Ministry, p. 78

The Vision of a Parish's Social Ministry

Direct Service
Helping people survive their present crisis

Social Change
Addressing the root causes of social problems

Advocacy
Speaking for those who have no voice
- Lobby for funding for needed programs
- Educate the public on policy issues
- Legislation: Write or speak to legislators on current bills
- Voter registration

Organizing and Development
People organized for effective action in the public arena
- One-on-one relationship building
- Grassroots fundraising
- Grassroots issue identification and action
- Leadership training

Charity and Outreach
Providing the basic necessities to help people survive in the existing system
- Food pantries
- Clothing centers
- Visiting the elderly, shut-ins, prisoners
- Provide cultural opportunities for disadvantaged youth

Solidarity
Living with and for the oppressed, empowering the oppressed and provoking personal conversion
- Justice and peace activities
- Sister communities
- Sponsor a family
- Live among the poor

The whole picture allows for a more complete vision.

IV. Skill Development: Program Development
Goal: practice planning methodology; develop skills in program analysis
    A. Large Group Discussion
        1. Review of Program Development process
        2. Introduction to the analysis
    B. Meet in small groups of four or five people.
        1. The problem will be named for you.
        2. Anticipate moving through steps A and B of the Program Development outline (i.e., identifying the issue and defining the goal) quickly.
        3. Give adequate time to brainstorming; be as creative as possible. Focus on strategies that will take you "up the river."
        4. Spend the majority of time on the analysis; think through what it might take to implement such a strategy. Take good notes.
    C. Large Group Summary
        1. Small groups state their goal and several of their best strategies to the large group.
        2. Facilitator walks through the remaining steps in Program Development (decision-making, implementation, and evaluation) *(see "Program Development," p. 68)*

PREPARATION FOR SESSION 6:
THE DIGNITY OF WORK AND THE RIGHTS OF WORKERS

- *Meet* with your pastor or staff representative; *listen* to his or her ideas about the social mission of your parish.
- *Write* a brief reflection on ways in which you can work with the pastor or staff to expand the social mission of your parish.
- *Read*
    - From "Communities of Salt and Light": *The Dignity of Work and the Rights of Workers*
    - Article, *An Introduction to Congregation-Based Organizing*, p. 168
- *Complete* the Rights and Responsibilities Quadrants.

Advocacy

What are we already doing for the theme of
Rights and Responsibilities in the area of
Advocacy?
1.
2.
3.

What else could we be doing?
1.
2.
3.

Organizing

What are we already doing for the theme of
Rights and Responsibilities in the area of
Organizing and Development?
1.
2.
3.

What else could we be doing?
1.
2.
3.

Rights and Responsibilities

Charity

What are we already doing for the theme of
Rights and Responsibilities in the area of
Charity and Outreach?
1.
2.
3.

What else could we be doing?
1.
2.
3.

Solidarity

What are we already doing for the theme of
Rights and Responsibilities in the area of
Solidarity and Community Building?
1.
2.
3.

What else could we be doing?
1.
2.
3.

SESSION 5 RESOURCES
"Faithful Citizenship"
The USCCB's statement and resources on faithful citizenship are updated every year before the presidential election.

Web sites:
Catholic Charities USA /Social Policy Department
www.catholiccharitiesusa.org
United States Conference of Catholic Bishops www.usccb.org (Faithful Citizenship Resources)
USCCB/Social Development & World Peace www.usccb.org/sdwp
Catholic Relief Services/Church Outreach www.catholicrelief.org
NETWORK: A Social Justice Lobby www.networklobby.org
State Catholic Conferences
www.nasccd.org/StateConferences/Websitetable.htm

HUMAN RIGHTS
United Nations www.un.org

SKILL BUILDING: VISION OF PARISH SOCIAL MINISTRY
Parish Social Ministry: Strategies for Success, Tom Ulrich, (Ave Maria Press, 1-800-282-1865, www.avemariapress.com)
Resources from the United States Conference of Catholic Bishops:
800-235-8722
www.usccb.org
"Communities of Salt and Light: Reflections on the Social Mission of the Parish"
English: No. 701-4, 24 pp.
Spanish: No. 724-3, 24 pp.
"Communities of Salt and Light: Parish Resource Manual"
No. 702-2, 80 pp.
"Called to Global Solidarity: International Challenges for U.S. Parishes"
English: No. 5-118; 48 pp.
Spanish: No. 5-119; 56 pp.
"Global Solidarity" (Videotape)
A Framework for Parishes
No. 5-272, 14 minutes

Building Peace and Justice, Roberta Ann Leskey, C.S.B. and Lucianne Siers, O.P. (Center for Learning Network, 800-767-9090)

Social Analysis: Linking Faith and Justice, Joe Holland and Peter Henriot, S.J. (Orbis Books, 800-258-5838, www.maryknollmall.org)

THE DIGNITY OF WORK AND THE RIGHTS OF WORKERS

AGENDA
- Prayer
- Recap/Overview
  - What did you learn from your conversation with your pastor and/or staff?
- Catholic Social Teaching: The Dignity of Work and the Rights of Workers
- Scriptural Basis for Community Organizing
- Congregation-Based Organizing
- Break
- Skill Development: Volunteer Recruitment and One-on-One Interviews
- Preparation for Session 7: Solidarity
- Evaluation: Oral
- Closing Prayer

Catholic Social Teaching:
The Dignity of Work and the Rights of Workers[16]
Goal: develop an understanding of the role and development of rights of workers in Catholic social teaching

I. *Rerum Novarum*: "On the Condition of Labor," Pope Leo XIII, 1891
  A. Set the stage for the church to place itself firmly in the midst of the burning social questions of the day
    1. Laid a solid foundation on which later social teachings could be built—both in content and character
    2. A cry of protest against exploitation of poor workers
  B. Built upon foundation of human dignity and dignity of work and developed specific worker's rights
    1. Included: sufficient wages to support a family, freedom to receive and spend wages as the workers see fit, etc.
    2. Upheld basic rights of proper sanitation, hours, etc.

II. *Quadragesimo Anno*: "On Restructuring the Social Order," Pope Pius XI, 1931
  A. Reviewed impact of *Rerum Novarum* and reiterated its themes
    1. Advocated on behalf of the common good
    2. Proposed just wages, profit-sharing; shared ownership
  B. Introduced a critically important concept in the development of CST: Subsidiarity "Just as it is gravely wrong to take from individuals what they can accomplish by their own initiative and industry and give it to the community, so also it is an injustice and at the same time a grave evil and disturbance of right order to assign to a greater and higher association what lesser and subordinate organizations can do."
    1. Applies the concept to the state, emphasizing that larger political entities should not absorb the functions of smaller, more local ones; also points out that the state must act when smaller entities are unable to adequately address the problem.
    2. It insists that all parties work in ways that build up society as reflects their distinctive capacities; it underscores importance of families, neighborhood associations, community organizations, etc., as well as local, state, national, *and* international government.
    3. Ultimately, the principle is rooted in human dignity . . . we are most human and responsive when we make decisions and solve problems as close to the people affected by them as possible.

III. *Laborem Exercens*: "On Human Work," Pope John Paul II, 1981
  A. Work is at the center of social question.
      1. Work furthers the creative design and activity of God.
      2. A redistribution of work is called for to achieve "suitable employment for all who are capable of it,"—and appropriate provisions must be made for those who are unable to work.
  B. Work is the key to making life more human and the measure of human dignity.
      1. People are "the subjects of work" (rather than tools or objects in the productive process).
      2. Labor and the rights of all laborers developed in the previous encyclicals are affirmed and strengthened.

SCRIPTURAL BASIS FOR COMMUNITY ORGANIZING
Goal: develop an understanding of the scriptural basis for community organizing

I. Jesus is baptized (Lk 3:21–23)
  A. Jesus is called to ministry and begins his public life

II. Jesus rejects false power (Lk 4:1–13); presents God's kingdom on earth (Lk 14:16–19)
  A. Jesus rejects domination, or "power over" others. Why?
      1. The devil's offer represents another layer of "power over"
          a) Others would be in debt to Jesus, and Jesus in debt to the devil: unilateral control
          b) Promotes a world based on dependence, not trust; control, not mutuality
          c) Homage, not faith and values, as source for action
      2. Jesus came to build community, love, justice
          a) Jesus is the living message of God
          b) Faith, values, discipleship as purpose for action
  B. Jesus acknowledges the reality and humanness of temptation.
      1. Models rejection to temptation for faith in God and God's Kingdom
          a) Calls us to reject the temptation to false power of prestige and control

b) Calls us to trust in the power of God

2. Calls each of us as disciples into public life through baptism to actively struggle with the tension between power and justice.

III. Jesus seeks to build God's kingdom on earth.
   A. Jesus builds his base (Mt 4:18–22; Mk 1:14–22; Lk 5:1–11)
      1. Approached individuals, one-on-one, and asked them personally to "come, follow me"
         a) Saw leadership potential in the "everyday" person
         b) Did not seek people in power, rather people with values and a sense of self and other
         c) Sought to expand their own interest in others, in the common good
   B. Jesus develops a leadership base: Jesus' ministry in Galilee and Perea
      1. Leadership training and development
         a) Major part of Jesus' time, up to his turn to Jerusalem
         b) Teaches in parables and defines the Kingdom of God
         c) Models leadership and action rooted in love—roots ministry in prayer, relationships, values
      2. Establishes a structure through which the work may continue: church, leadership (disciples), and mission
   C. Establishes the Golden Rule: (Mt 7:12)
      1. "Treat others the way you would have them treat you"
      2. Essentially, combines the first two commandments
         a) "Love God above all else."
         b) That love demands that you "Do unto others as you would have done unto you."

IV. Jesus defines his/our mission
   A. **Conflict:** "My mission is to spread, not peace, but division." (cf. Mt 10:34–40)
      1. We are called to *shake the roots of complacency* and challenge the status quo;
         a) To "wage war" against poverty, misery, injustice, hopelessness, and despair;
         b) To be *ardent in our pursuit of justice.*

2. Jesus' primary focus for change was the established leadership,
   a) Held all individuals—poor, prostitutes, etc.—accountable for their own actions
   b) Sought to uproot and break down existing structures and replace them with more just systems
B. **Accountability:** "Deny your very selves, take up your cross, and begin to follow in my footsteps." (cf. Mt 16:24–28)
   1. We are challenged to let go of what we know in the present (what we can see, taste, etc.), and trust in what we say we believe.
      a) Jesus calls us to be accountable to our faith.
      b) Can we risk worldly safety, security, etc., for a more just system? For a most just world?
   2. Jesus challenges the heart of current faith practices with a more genuine belief rooted in love.
C. **Humility:** "You who aspire to greatness must serve the rest." (Mk 10:35–45)
   1. Jesus challenges us to be on guard against faulty ambitions.
      a) The work of building the Kingdom is about building the esteem, the talents, the abilities, the *power* of others, especially the "least."
      b) It is not in the acquisition of power, but in the lived tension of power and justice that the Kingdom is realized.
   2. Everyone plays a part in building the Kingdom; no one person, or group of people, has a monopoly on the truth.
      a) It is in the collective work of building relationships that we experience the reign of God.
      b) Our faith is profoundly social.
D. **Empowerment:** "Blest will you be if you put them into practice." (Jn 13:1–17)
   1. Jesus models service to all by washing his disciples' feet.
      a) Love that which is most human
      b) Serve in humility to all . . . to prepare others for service
   2. Jesus empowers disciples to fulfill the church's mission through simple, loving acts.

CONGREGATION-BASED ORGANIZING
Goal: identify the basic elements of congregation-based organizing

I. Recognition of and answer to our baptismal call to discipleship—A means of living out our faith in the public arena

II. Rejection of false power
    A. Acknowledgement of the need for structural change
    B. Commitment to build the Kingdom of God on earth
       1. It is in the process of building, of forming relationships, that we experience the Kingdom.
       2. It is in the breaking of the bread that we know Jesus.

III. Build Base
    A. Emphasis on *Relationship Building*
       1. One-on-one with genuine interest in the other: *Listening*
       2. Not a selfish pursuit for self gain; rather, an act of love
          a) That is, relationships are not a means to an end (power), but the end in itself.
    B. Develop *Leadership*
       1. Drawn from "everyday" people—moderates of self and others
       2. Rooted in one's experience, values, sense of self and others
       3. Potential blossoms out of one's joys, sorrows, passions, angers, etc.
       4. Great emphasis on finding and training new leaders—broadening the base
          a) Prevent dependence on a few (over the many)
          b) Challenge the many to assume rightful responsibility
    C. Iron Rule
       1. "*Never* do for others what they can do for themselves."
       2. Loving translation of the Golden Rule
          a) Rooted in respect for human dignity
          b) Fundamentally, echoes the principle of subsidiarity

IV. Mission: To build "power with"
    A. Old adage: "If you want peace, work for justice; if you want justice, build power."

1. Rooted in our baptismal call to action, stewardship
2. Again, echoes the principle of subsidiarity
B. Elements of congregation-based organizing
   1. **Conflict**
      a) Shake the roots of complacency; challenge the status quo
      b) Ardent pursuit of justice
   2. **Accountability**
      a) Hold each other accountable to act on one's values and beliefs
      b) Loving stance assumed only when in right relationship with another
   3. **Humility**
      a) A process of building relationships for the sake of relationships; power; justice—not for one's own ambitions
      b) Rather than a selfish pursuit, organizing promotes an "enlightened self interest"—action on behalf of all
   4. **Empowerment**
      a) Love and challenge others to develop their gifts for the pursuit of justice
      b) Live out your beliefs and in so doing model appropriate action
   5. **Action**

SKILL DEVELOPMENT:
VOLUNTEER RECRUITMENT AND ONE-ON-ONE INTERVIEWS

Goal: develop skills in volunteer recruitment, in particular the one-on-one interview

I. Volunteer recruitment
   A. Overview
      1. Every organization needs to recruit new members to survive and grow.
      2. While some people will initiate joining an organization on their own, most need to be invited to participate by someone with whom they have a personal relationship.
      3. Recruiting needs to be focused on the intentional, proactive, and systemic building of new relationships.

4. Brainstorm ways to recruit volunteers
   a) Ask face to face
   b) Call them on the phone
   c) Have a priest or staff member offer an invitation
   d) Offer rewards/incentives
   e) Hold an open house—table display
   f) Education on the topic
   g) Nominate, inform, and then vote someone in
   e) Make announcements from the pulpit and in the bulletin, newsletters, flyers
   f) Use referrals
   g) Write letters and follow up with face-to-face meetings

B. Discuss effectiveness of recruitment tactics and the purpose of recruitment
   1. Distinction: For what are you recruiting: *your* program or to engage people in the social mission of the church?
   2. Purpose will govern tactic

II. The One-on-One Interview[17]
   A. Definition
      1. Methodology of initiating, creating, and nurturing relationships
      2. Must be able to take person where they are at *and* not leave them there
      3. Primary tool of church-based community organizations to build a base of power rooted in values and a common self interest
   B. Purpose
      1. To find new leaders within the congregation
      2. To involve more individuals and families in the social mission of the church
      3. To uncover the concerns, interests, and needs of the parishioners in order to better create an action agenda that reflects the needs and interests of the parishioners
   C. Structure
      1. Time frame: Each interview should last 30–40 minutes
      2. Preparation
         a) Must ask yourself—why am I conducting this interview?

            (1) To introduce yourself, if you have not already done so

            (2) To develop the relationship

            (3) To create some sense of legitimacy or credential for you and your committee

            (4) To get a second meeting

     b) *Whom* will you be interviewing?

            (1) Key leaders in the parish: pastor, other clergy and religious, parish staff, parish council members, other "informal" leaders

            (2) People recommended to you by these leaders and your own committee

     c) Make an appointment, generally by phone

            (1) *Key* elements of the phone conversation: who you are; who you work with (committee); who suggested that you call; why you called (your purpose); and to request 30 minutes of their time. Identify your purpose as to listen to their concerns and hopes for the church, social mission, etc.

            (2) If a committee member already has a relationship with the person you are pursuing, that person should hold the interview.

            (3) Set the appointment; *do not start the interview over the phone!*

3. The interview

     a) Credential—5 minutes

            (1) Restate your name, committee or place of work, who recommended that you meet this person, and why you are here

     b) Focus—20 minutes

            (1) The meat of the interview

            (2) Uncover concerns, passions, a sense of the other by talking and listening

            (3) Begin by talking briefly about yourself and some of your concerns (e.g., why you are on X committee, or why you work for the parish, etc.)

            (4) Soon, turn the conversation to the person: what are your concerns? What would you like to see happen in this parish?

(5) Get to know the person and their self-interest; ask, "How do these problems, pressures, or lack of values affect you? The parish? Why do you think these things happen?"

(6) While you may share some personal things, you do *not* want to meddle into their private affairs.

(7) Should the meeting go longer than the thirty minutes, ask permission to take more of their time.

(8) Always convey a professional image of yourself—you want to be taken seriously and want the other person to know that he or she will be taken seriously.

(9) *Do* not *take notes*; if you must write something down, ask permission.

c) Next Steps—5 minutes

(1) Two essential follow-up questions:

(2) May I call you again to pursue this discussion? When?

(3) Is there anyone else that you think I should talk with?

(4) On a second visit, challenge him or her to come to the next meeting.

(5) You may find that the person's interests lie more in another area; suggest that she or he talk with a leader from the appropriate committee and ask if you may give that leader her or his name.

4. Evaluation

a) Take fifteen minutes after the interview to reflect on what happened.

b) *Write down* (either on your own form or an index card) pertinent factual information about the person (i.e., name, address, family info, brief biography, experience in ministry, skills, interesting personal qualities).

c) Keep a file of all interviewees.

d) Be sure to follow through on anything that you said you would do in the meeting.

D. Constituency—Whom do you need to be in relationship with?

1. Leaders—people who are respected and trusted in the parish and/or community

a) Possess a profound belief in others (not just one's own glorification).

b) Maintain values as the basis for action; be willing to act decisively when values are violated.

c) Have a good sense of humor.

d) Have a genuine curiosity about the world and life.

e) Includes clergy, laity, and staff

   (1) Must continually ask yourself how strong your relationships are with key parish leaders

2. Workers—people who are willing to follow through on tasks or projects

   a) Strong sense of duty; diligence

   b) Shows initiative; interest; willingness to learn

   c) Team player

PREPARATION FOR SESSION 7: SOLIDARITY

- *Read*
  - "Communities of Salt and Light": *Building Solidarity: Beyond Parish Boundaries*
  - Article, *The Service of the Poor and Spiritual Growth*, Albert Nolan, OP, p. 176
  - Section on meeting facilitation, p. 103
- *Complete*
  - Sections A and B, and begin D, of the Parish Assessment and Personal Action Plan, p. 184
  - The Worker Justice Quadrants, p. 94

Advocacy

What are we already doing for the theme of *Dignity of Work* in the area of Advocacy?

1.
2.
3.

What else could we be doing?

1.
2.
3.

Organizing

What are we already doing for the theme of *Dignity of Work* in the area of Organizing and Development?

1.
2.
3.

What else could we be doing?

1.
2.
3.

Worker Justice (Dignity of Work)

Charity

What are we already doing for the theme of *Dignity of Work* in the area of Charity and Outreach?

1.
2.
3.

What else could we be doing?

1.
2.
3.

Solidarity

What are we already doing for the theme of *Dignity of Work* in the area of Solidarity and Community Building?

1.
2.
3.

What else could we be doing?

1.
2.
3.

SESSION 6 RESOURCES

Workers Rights Issues

National Interfaith Committee for Worker Justice
www.nicwj.org/index.html

The Catholic Labor Network www.catholiclabor.org/home.htm

John A. Ryan Institute for Catholic Social Thought
www.stthomas.edu/cathstudies/cst/index.html

Human Rights for Workers www.senser.com

"Yo Trabajo la Tierra" (I Work the Land) (Videotape)
This portrait of a migrant family is a visual meditation on the dignity
of work and faith. Minimal dialogue in Spanish with English subtitles,
the program includes a bilingual study guide.
800-235-8722
www.usccb.org
No. 472-4, 13 minutes

COMMUNITY ORGANIZING

Cold Anger, Beth Rogers (University of North Texas Press, 1990)

*Building Communities from the Inside Out: A Path Toward Finding and
Mobilizing a Community's Assets*, John Kretzmann and John McKnight
(ACTA, 800-397-2282)

SKILLS: ONE-ON-ONE INTERVIEWS & RECRUITING VOLUNTEERS

Parish Social Ministry: Strategies for Success, Tom Ulrich (Ave Maria Press,
800-282-1865, www.avemariapress.com)

Training for Transformation, Anne Hope, Sally Timmel, and Chris Hodzi.
Process used to organize Christian communities in South Africa.
(Stylus Publications, 1996)

Web sites:

The Catholic Campaign for Human Development
www.usccb.org/cchd/index.htm

The Roundtable: Association of Diocesan Social Action Directors—
document on Community Organizing www.nplc.org/roundtable.htm

Pacific Institute of Community Organizing www.piconetwork.org

Direct Action and Research www.thedartcenter.org

Gamaliel Foundation www.gamaliel.org/Foundation/foundation.htm

Industrial Areas Foundation—The On-Line Conference on Community
Organizing and Development comm-org.utoledo.edu

SESSION 7:

SOLIDARITY

AGENDA
- Prayer: "The Road Ahead" by Thomas Merton, or a similar prayer
- Recap/Overview
  - What struck you about Albert Nolan's article?
  - How did it affect your perspective of the past weeks together?
- Catholic Social Teaching : Solidarity
  - History and Purpose
  - Large Group Discussion: Why work on solidarity? How do you build it?
- Skill Development: Leadership
  - Large group presentation: Leadership Qualities and Styles
  - Completion of the Personal Action Plan (p. 184)
- Break
- Skill Development: Facilitation and Effective Meetings
  - Small Group Exercise: "How to Run a Meeting"
- Evaluation: Written and Oral
- Closing Prayer Service: "Living and Dying in Solidarity"

CATHOLIC SOCIAL TEACHING: SOLIDARITY[18]

Goals: (1) develop an understanding of our own spiritual development in relation to the poor, (2) develop a sense of the progression of Catholic social teaching and the role solidarity plays in that progression

I. Shifts in Catholic social teaching
   A. Dominant social perspective
      1. Early social teaching assumed an autocratic, Euro-Western focus; southern or third-world countries remained on the periphery of dominant social thought.
      2. Gradual shift toward a new world order with the southern countries at center focus
         a) Call for the development and participation of poor nations, and the poor themselves, in the transformation of their own lives and the world
         b) Rather than advocate one or another social system, church now assumes a prophetic stance vis-à-vis all systems
   B. Connection of faith and the social question
      1. Social reality (be it plight of the workers, the poor, or of poor nations) shifts from the application of one's faith to the center of the faith question.
         a) Preferential love for the poor is seen as central to the church's understanding of both God and Christ.
      2. As suggested by the prophets, the quality of our faith is measured by the quality of justice in the land.
         a) Justice is recognized to be central to the proclamation of the gospel; the doing of justice is central to both evangelization and liberation.
         b) *Without the doing of justice, God remains unknown.*

II. *Sollicitudo Rei Socialis*: "The Social Concerns of the Church," 1987
   A. Written on the twentieth anniversary of Pope Paul VI's *Populorum Progresso*: "On the Development of Peoples," 1967
   B. Contrasts Pope Paul's hope for development with the worsening realities of underdevelopment and the widening division between first and third world realities

C. Interdependence
   1. While our biblical roots suggest inherent interdependence, present day reality suggests an ever increasing global interconnectedness in terms of media, science, economics, the environment, and politics.
      a) Transnational problem with transnational actors
      b) The problem is not interdependence, but our failure to tend to it.
   2. Solidarity becomes the "appropriate Christian response" to our interdependent reality.

   "In a world divided and beset by every type of conflict, the conviction is growing of a radical interdependence and consequently of the need for a *Solidarity* which will take up interdependence and transfer it to the moral plane. . . . The idea is slowly emerging that the good to which we are called and the happiness to which we aspire cannot be obtained without an effort and commitment on the part of all, nobody excluded, and the consequent renouncing of personal selfishness" (#26, emphasis added).

D. Solidarity
   1. As suggested above, Pope John Paul II strengthened the concept by raising it to a "moral category," a virtue

   "Solidarity is not a feeling of vague compassion or shallow distress at the misfortunes of so many people. On the contrary, it is a firm and persevering determination to commit oneself to the common good; that is to say, to the good of all and of each individual because we are all really responsible for all" (#38, emphasis added).

E. Pope John Paul clarifies solidarity as the Christian commitment—of the rich to share their goods and services; of the poor to assert their rights; and for all to seek a mutual cooperation in developing a more just world:

   "The exercise of *Solidarity* within each society is valid when its members recognize one another as persons. Those who are more influential because they have a greater share of goods and common services should feel responsible for the weaker and be ready to share with them all they possess. Those who are weaker, for their part, in the same spirit of solidarity should not adopt a purely passive attitude or one that is destructive of the social fabric, but while claiming their legitimate rights should do what they can for the good of all" (#39, emphasis added).

1. He echoes Pope Paul's famous claim: "development is the new name for peace":

"The *Solidarity* that we propose is the path to peace and at the same time to development. For world peace is inconceivable unless the world leaders come to recognize that interdependence in itself demands the abandonment of the politics of blocs, the sacrifice of all forms of economic, military or political imperialism and the transformation of mutual distrust into collaboration. This is precisely the act proper to solidarity among individuals and nations" (39.7, emphasis added).

2. Solidarity goes beyond charity:

"In the light of faith, *Solidarity* seeks to go beyond itself, to take on the specifically Christian dimensions of total gratuity, forgiveness and reconciliation. One's neighbor is then not only a human being with his or her own rights and a fundamental equality with everyone else, but becomes the living image of God the Father, redeemed by the blood of Jesus Christ and placed under the permanent action of the Holy Spirit. One's neighbor must therefore be loved, even if an enemy, with the same love with which the Lord loves him or her; and for that person's sake one must be ready for sacrifice, even the ultimate one: to lay down one's life for the brethren" (#40.1, emphasis added).

III. Large Group Discussion
   A. What does it mean to work towards solidarity in our lives, our parish, our neighborhood?
   B. How do you build solidarity?

SKILL DEVELOPMENT: LEADERSHIP[19]

We often think of a leader as a person who is smart or well educated, or someone who is articulate or who can run a meeting well. These are nice skills for a leader to possess, but they are not the essential qualities of a leader.

God chose a man with a speech impediment (Moses) as the leader to free the Israelites. He chose an uneducated fisherman (Peter) to build his church. Both protested to God at first.

They were both unlikely choices, but both possessed important leadership qualities. The following are some valuable qualities for a leader:

Risk-Taker	If you have come to terms with your own death then you can take risks. This coming to terms is done by dealing with the death of someone close to you or with mini-deaths, disappointments, and grief experiences. These experiences make some people stronger while others collapse. Being in touch with your death can change your action. You don't have to be liked because you have nothing to lose.
Healthy Anger	The root of anger is *angr* which means *grief*, or loss. Thus anger stems from a loss of what was (memory) or what could be (vision). A leader is in touch with his or her anger, reflects on it, works with it, and channels it to positive ends.
Possesses a Sense of Humor	A leader has the ability to maintain perspective, to sit back, look, and laugh. A healthy sense of humor enables the leader to enjoy his or her work, and find a balance between cynicism and self-righteousness.
Courageous	A leader is willing to accept challenges and take risks. As the saying goes, "Nothing ventured, nothing gained."
Agitator	A leader stirs things up. People will not be the same after being with this person. You can't get clothes cleaned without an agitator!

Self-Aware	A leader is clear on his or her self-interest; only then can she or he appreciate the interests of others. Because of the clarity, the leader can compromise, negotiate, and make commitments.
Vision and Values	Good leaders are clear about their values and have some idea about what they would like the world to be. A group leader is willing to stand up and work to make those values and that vision become a reality.
Accountability	A good leader is able to hold others accountable to their commitments and is willing to be held accountable by others. A good leader lives up to commitments and is interested in reciprocal relationships.
Trusts People	Leaders trust that given the opportunity, people tend to do the right thing. A good leader shares power and responsibility and encourages others to develop their talents. She or he allows people to make mistakes and abides by the "iron rule": *Never do for others what they can do for themselves.*
Cares for Others	Good leaders are curious. They get inside people's skin. Successful leaders meet others because they care about people.
Possesses Imagination	Good leaders rely on their imagination to identify issues that are hidden or obscure, and to find effective responses to issues that have never been tried before.

> **Good leaders are not born as leaders; they are developed. Anyone can become a leader.**

Skill Development: Facilitation and Effective Meetings

I. Purpose of an Effective Meeting
    A. Make an important decision or ratify a course of action—*Primary*
        1. Decisions require presence for input and votes
        2. All too often, meetings are held simply to share information.
            a) Information can be shared informally, through minutes or bulletins, or over the phone.
            b) Information does not require physical or mental presence
    B. Prayer and fellowship—community building—*Secondary*
        1. Community building is important for an effective committee.
        2. Can be a part of regular meetings (i.e., prayer at beginning/end; fellowship after the meeting concludes) and/or separate "retreat days" where this purpose is stated explicitly

II. Preparation
    A. Agenda—a tool for planning
        1. Committee leaders meet to plan agenda ahead of time
            a) Will flow from previous meetings' "next steps" and discussion among committee leaders
            b) Should be mailed to participants about one week before meeting
                (1) Participants and leaders come to meeting fully informed
                (2) No surprises
    B. Turnout
        1. Responsibility of those planning the meeting and involves:
            a) Planning the agenda
            b) Personal contact with members
        2. Successful turnout depends upon:
            a) An agenda that reflects the participants' self-interest
            b) Participants' relationship with committee leaders

III. The Meeting
    A. Agenda—an accountability tool
        1. Highlights the major focus of the meeting by its placement and time allotted on the agenda
            a) An effective meeting should have one (at most, two) highlights
            b) The highlight is what the planners want the participants to discuss and bring back to their parish, committee, constituency

2. Guides the meeting
   a) While the agenda is mailed in advance to help people prepare for the meeting, the agenda must be adopted at the meeting
      (1) The people must agree to: the business to be conducted; the time period within which it will be conducted; and, who will present/chair the discussion
      (2) Members can amend agenda
   b) Once adopted by the group, it is *the plan* for the meeting
B. Facilitation
   1. Chairperson has two primary responsibilities
      a) Unity of the meeting: maintain/foster members' ownership of the meeting and the decisions made
      b) Accomplish the purpose of the meeting
         (1) By keeping to the agenda
         (2) If the group strays, ask if they want to stick to the agenda or amend it.
   2. Chairperson's role must be:
      a) **Legitimate**—whether elected or appointed, chairperson's authority ultimately comes from the people
      b) **Fair**—chairperson must treat all members fairly
      c) **Firm**—chairperson keeps to the agenda
C. Participation
   1. Members come prepared to discuss issue at hand and employ discipline to stick to their point
   2. Members help chairperson move meeting along by supporting the purpose of the meeting and respecting people's time and opinions
D. Next steps and evaluation
   1. Once a decision is made, the next steps are decided
      a) What needs to be done to accomplish the goal?
      b) Who is going to do X, Y, or Z and in what time frame? The next meeting begins with a report on actions taken.
   2. Evaluation follows the meeting
      a) Time for learning
      b) Honest critique: Did we start/end on time? What did we accomplish? Did everyone participate? etc.

IV. Sample agenda

Time in minutes	Agenda Item
5	Welcome and introductions
5-15	Prayer
5	Adopt minutes of previous meeting Adopt agenda
1-5	Comments from chairperson
10-15	Brief reports (as needed): financial, update from "next steps" taken
30–40	*Highlight*: focus of meeting one (at most, two) decision(s) to be made
10	Next steps Adjournment Evaluation

FACILITATING A MEETING

Good Facilitation Tactics	Bad Facilitation Tactics
Follows the agenda	Disregards the agenda
Summarizes discussion as the meeting progresses	Monopolizes the meeting or remains aloof to discussion
Moderates discussion	Railroads issues
Good timing	Too rigid or too loose
Assertive, not aggressive	Hesitant; doesn't know procedures
Follows basic parliamentary procedures	Changes rules midstream
Solicits from those who are not speaking; utilizes resources in the group	Selective in recognizing people
Prevents monopoly	Allows a few to dominate the meeting
Maintains objectivity	Subjective positions influence facilitation
Provides pertinent information	Listless; offers no constructive input
Informed decision-making; well prepared	Arbitrary decision-making; ill-prepared
Open to constructive criticism	Easily offended; big ego, or too sensitive
Clear and articulate	Inarticulate—mumbles, wordy, etc.
Punctual; dependable	Late; irregular
Able to read the group	Unaware; dense
Appropriate use of humor, story telling	Humorless, impersonal

BECOMING A COMMUNITY OF SALT AND LIGHT

FACILITATIVE LISTENING SKILLS[20]

1. **Questioning**—seeks additional information by using open-ended
   questions that encourage the speaker to continue to speak; avoid questions with yes/no answers, or
   simply asking "Why?"
   a. "What do you think might have led to that conclusion?"
   b. "Could you give us more explanation on that?"

2. **Clarifying**—seeks clarity on a point by asking a question or repeating a point in different words
   a. "I'm not sure I understand . . ."
   b. "Are you saying . . ."

3. **Reflecting**—allows the speaker to hear both feelings and content
   a. "It sounds like you feel/think . . . because . . ."

4. **Understanding**—conveys empathy (as opposed to sympathy)
   a. "It must be difficult for you to . . ."
   b. "That must really have made an impact on you."

5. **Summarizing**—seeks to put together the major ideas and feelings that have come out in the discussion
   a. "It sounds like the group agrees on . . . but finds little consensus on . . ."

6. **Body language**—nonverbally conveys that you are listening
   a. Eye contact, nodding, sitting forward and turning your body to the speaker.
   b. Every now and then, check your body language. Are you making eye contact, sitting forward, etc? If not,
      ask yourself whether you really are listening to the speaker. More than likely you are not. Good body
      language does not only *convey* that you are listening; it *helps* you to listen better.

Final Evaluation, p. 157

CLOSING PRAYER SERVICE
LIVING AND DYING IN SOLIDARITY

Quieting Time
Opening Prayer:

> Loving God, Sophia—Spirit of Wisdom,
> All creation calls you blessed!
> Your breath imprints the whole universe with life and mystery,
> With vision and promise.
> O Giver of Hope, send us your spirit
> Create in our hearts the desire to embrace all creation!
> Amen.

Reading: John 15:9–17
Moment of Meditation

Narrator:

> Four American church women, Ita Ford, Dorothy Kazel, Maura Clarke, and Jean Donovan responded to God's call to be one with the poor of El Salvador. Aware that the depth of their compassion and commitment could cost them their lives, they freely chose not only to live with and for the people of El Salvador, but also to die with them.
>
> On December 2, 1980, they were brutally tortured and murdered by members of El Salvador's national guard. Through the memory and witness of the life and death of Ita, Dorothy, Maura, and Jean, may we respond to God's continuing call to solidarity with the poor.

Reader 1:

> Am I willing to suffer with the people here, the suffering of the powerless, the feeling impotent? Can I say to my neighbors—I have no solutions to this situation; I don't know the answers, but I will walk with you, search with you, be with you. Can I let myself be evangelized by this opportunity? Can I look at and accept my own poorness as I learn from the poor ones? —Ita Ford

Reader 2:

> We talked quite a bit today about what happens if something begins. And most of us feel we would want to stay here. Now this depends on what happens—if there is a way we can help—like run a refugee center or something. We wouldn't want to just run out on the people. . . . I thought I should say this to you cuz I don't want to say it to anyone else—cuz I don't think they would understand. Anyway my beloved friend, just know how I feel and "treasure it in your heart." If a day comes when others will have to understand, please explain it for me. —Dorothy Kazel

Reader 3:

> I am beginning to see death in a new way. We have been meditating a lot on death and the accepting of it, as in the Good Shepherd reading. There are so many deaths everywhere that it is incredible. It is an

atmosphere of death. The work is really what Archbishop Romero calls "acompanamiento," accompanying the people, as well as searching for ways to help. This seems to be what the Lord is asking of me, I think at this moment. We are on the road continually, bringing women and children to refugee centers. Keep us in your heart and prayers, especially the poor forsaken people. —Maura Clarke

Reader 4:

I love life and I love living. While I feel compassion and cry for the people here, I'm not up for suicide. . . . Several times I decided to leave. I almost could, except for the children—the poor, bruised victims of this adult lunacy. Who would care for them? Whose heart could be so staunch as to favor the reasonable thing in a sea of their tears and loneliness? Not mine dear friend, not mine. —Jean Donovan

Facilitator:

These four women lived out their baptismal call by living and dying with their brothers and sisters in El Salvador. Over the last six sessions of the *Becoming a Community of Salt and Light* training, you have had the opportunity to reflect on your own baptismal call in the social mission of the church. Take a few minutes in quiet reflection with your neighbor; discuss:

1. *One* way you have grown or changed from your experience in the *Salt and Light* training program.
2. *One* action you will take because of this growth or change.

Listen to your partner's story as well. You will have about five minutes.

Large Group Sharing of Reflection

Blessing:

May God bless you and keep you.
May God's face shine upon you, and be gracious to you.
And may God look upon you with kindness and give you peace.
Amen.

Closing Song

Advocacy

What are we already doing for the theme of *Solidarity* in the area of Advocacy?
1.
2.
3.

What else could we be doing?
1.
2.
3.

Organizing

What are we already doing for the theme of *Solidarity* in the area of Organizing and Development?
1.
2.
3.

What else could we be doing?
1.
2.
3.

Solidarity

Charity

What are we already doing for the theme of *Solidarity* in the area of Charity and Outreach?
1.
2.
3.

What else could we be doing?
1.
2.
3.

Solidarity

What are we already doing for the theme of *Solidarity* in the area of Solidarity and Community Building?
1.
2.
3.

What else could we be doing?
1.
2.
3.

SESSION 7 RESOURCES

RESOURCES FROM THE UNITED STATES CONFERENCE OF CATHOLIC BISHOPS:

800-235-8722

www.usccb.org

"Called to Global Solidarity: International Challenges for U.S. Parishes"
  English: No. 5-118; 48 pp.
  Spanish: No. 5-119; 56 pp.

"Global Solidarity" (Videotape)
  A Framework for Parishes
  No. 5-272, 14 minutes

"Welcoming the Stranger Among Us: Unity in Diversity" Kit
  The resources in this kit have been designed to offer practical
  guidance for building more welcoming and inclusive parishes. The kit
  contains copies of published documents and related resources (several
  of which can be photocopied and distributed to small groups and in
  other community settings). Included are:

  • Bishops' Statement "Welcoming the Stranger Among Us: Unity in
    Diversity"
  • Companion Brochure "Called to *Welcoming the Stranger Among Us*"
  • Camera-ready Brochure "Called to *Welcoming the Stranger Among
    Us*"
  • Prayer Card: "Welcoming the Stranger: A Prayer for Hospitality"
  • Letter and Planning Ideas for Pastors and Parish Leaders
  • Ideas for Liturgists and Prayer Leaders
  • Suggestions for Homilists
  • Ideas for Schools, Religious Education, and Youth Programs
  • Bulletin Quotes and Clip Art
  • A Guide to Understanding Catholic Social Teaching on Advocacy
    for Migrants and Refugees
  • Resource Bibliography
  • Order Form No. 5-407

"Welcoming the Stranger Among Us: Unity in Diversity"
  English: No. 5-375, 80 pp.
  Spanish: No. 5-848, 80 pp.

Unity in Diversity: A Scriptural Rosary

This brochure brings together two wonderful traditions of the Catholic Church—praying the rosary and celebrating unity within diversity. It includes prayers for the fifteen mysteries and instructions on praying the rosary. It focuses on the three themes of the U.S. bishops' statement, "Welcoming the Stranger Among Us: Unity in Diversity," conversion, communion, and solidarity. From the Office of Migration and Refugee Services.

English: No. 5-467, 8-panel brochure

Spanish: No. 5-870, 8-panel brochure

"Who Are My Sisters and Brothers?: Reflections for Understanding and Welcoming Immigrants and Refugees"

No. 5-057, 64 pp.

"Who Are My Sisters and Brothers?" (Videotape)

Understanding Immigrants and Refugees

No. 5-053, 27 minutes

"Called to One Table" prayer card

English: No. 5-484, card

Spanish: No. 5-869, card

"From Newcomers to Citizens: All Come Bearing Gifts"

No. 5-363, 12 pp.

Web sites:

Catholic Relief Services www.catholicrelief.org

Bread for the World www.bread.org

SKILLS: FACILITATION AND EFFECTIVE MEETINGS

National Pastoral Life Center—Follow Me Series

www.nplc.org/index.htm

Parish Social Ministry: Strategies for Success, Tom Ulrich (Ave Maria Press, 800-282-1865, www.avemariapress.com)

"Running Good Meetings," video (ACTA Publications, 800-397-2282, www.cbpa.org/publisher/acta.htm)

FORMING A COMMUNITY OF SALT AND LIGHT: FOLLOW-UP MEETING

PREPARATION:

Please look through and bring *Becoming a Community of Salt and Light.*

Review "Twenty Key Ideas" (pp. 188–189) and reflect on the following: Which quote strikes you the most and why? How is it relevant to what you would like to see continue from the *Salt and Light* course?

Review and complete the rating sheet on page 147.

AGENDA
- Opening Prayer
- Goals Discussion
  - Goals we met
  - Goals we didn't meet
  - Goals for the future: brainstorm and clarify
- Program Development
  - Problem
  - Analysis of Strategies
- Next Steps/Action
  Option one: Continue to explore CST themes.
  Option two: Perform a parish analysis of CST and parish life.
  Option three: Continue with program development
  Option four: Follow an original plan from the group.
- Closing Prayer: Salt and Light Prayer, p. 3

Follow-up Meeting

Opening Prayer

Scripture:

"You are the salt of the earth; but if salt has lost its taste, how can its flavor be restored? It is no longer good for anything, but is thrown out and trampled under foot.

"You are the light of the world. A city built on a hill cannot be hid. No one after lighting a lamp puts it under the bushel basket, but on the lamp-stand, and it gives light to all in the house. In the same way, let your light shine before others, so that they may see your good works and give glory to your Father in heaven" (Matthew 5:13–16).

Reflective Reading:

Leader: If we could shrink the earth's population to a village of precisely 100 people, with all the existing human ratios remaining the same, it would look something like the following. There would be:

- 57 Asians, 8 Africans, 21 Europeans, and 14 from the Western Hemisphere, both north and south
- 52 would be female, 48 would be male
- 70 would be non-white, 30 would be white
- 70 would be non-Christian, 30 would be Christian
- 89 would be heterosexual, 11 would be homosexual
- 6 would posses 59% of the entire world's wealth and all 6 would be from the United States
- 80 would live in substandard housing
- 70 would be unable to read
- 50 would suffer from malnutrition
- 1 (yes, only 1) would have a college education
- 1 would own a computer

All: In considering our world from such a compressed perspective, we see the obvious need for acceptance, understanding, and education and we pray for the courage and resourcefulness to "Think globally but act locally."

Leader: The following realities are also something to ponder:

- If you woke up this morning with more health than illness—you are more blessed than the million who will not survive this week.
- If you have never experienced the danger of battle, the loneliness of imprisonment, the agony of torture, or the pangs of starvation—you are ahead of 500 million people in the world.
- If you can attend a church meeting without fear of harassment, arrest, torture, or death—you are more blessed than three billion people in the world.
- If you have food in the refrigerator, clothes on your back, a roof overhead, and a place to sleep—you are richer than 75% of the world.

- If you have money in the bank, in your wallet, and spare change in a dish someplace—you are among the top 8% of the world's wealthy.
- If your parents are still alive and still married—you are very rare.
- If you hold up your head with a smile on your face and are truly thankful—you are blessed because the majority can, but most do not.
- If you can hold someone's hand, hug him or her, or even touch them on the shoulder—you are blessed because you can offer healing touch.
- If you can read this message you are more blessed than over two billion people in the world who cannot read at all.

All: Lord, we thank you for all our gifts and abundance. How we "serve the least of these" in our community and beyond is our challenge and our calling. We ask you to guide and inspire us to continually respond to our baptismal call as we seek to build a community of faith which upholds the social gospel.

Sharing:

From your review of Twenty Key Ideas (pp. 188 and 189) please share which quote or idea strikes you the most and why? How is this relevant to what you would like to see continue from the work we did with *Becoming a Community of Salt and Light?*

Conclusion:

All: Send your spirit upon us, O Lord! Anoint us for your mission to be salt and light for your kingdom. Bless our meeting and sharing today and this time we have together in your name, Amen.

PROGRAM DEVELOPMENT:

PROBLEM

Issue: Diagnose the problem into an issue that affects the parish/parishioners.

Goal: Come up with only one goal, although there may be many goals needed.

Strategies: Brainstorm many strategies for the one goal: What can the parish do?

Program Development Planning

1. **Issue**: _____
     Who _____
     What _____
     Where _____
2. **Goal**: _____
     Who _____
     What _____
     Where _____
3. **Strategies**: _____

Strategy:

Advantages	Disadvantages

Implementation of the Strategy

1. What is the "work" (what needs to be done)? Also where, when and how (if not already specified).

2. Who will do the work? Who oversees it/coordinates it?

3. Who is involved in decision? Who needs to be informed, consulted? Who approves or accepts it?

4. What are the resources needed?

5. What is success and how will we measure it?

FACILITATOR'S GUIDE

RECRUITMENT:

- Keep the size of the group to fifteen or sixteen people in order to tailor sessions to local needs and allow for good interaction.
- Pursue teams of *at least* two from a parish—four or more is best.
- Use existing networks to get the word out—clergy and lay, diocesan and parish-based, boards, commissions, parish councils, etc.; past participants ultimately are your best recruiters!
- Encourage parish recruiters to issue personal invitations.
- Send a letter to the pastors asking them to work with your other parish contacts to invite a team of leaders from the parish to participate in the training; include in the mailing a prepared bulletin announcement, if needed, and registration for the pastor to return to the training coordinator (you) with the participants' names, addresses, and phone numbers listed.
- In parishes, sponsor a condensed version of the training, one evening that will serve as a good adult education session as well as a recruitment tool.
- Draw on your own relationships with people from past events, one-on-one meetings, your own parish involvement, etc. and invite them personally.
- Send a mailing to the potential participants that includes: times, dates, and location of training; the overview sheets; the goals and objectives; and a commitment form that she or he must return to you.
- Send a second mailing to the participants with the bishops' statement, "Communities of Salt and Light," and reflection questions (e.g., what do you want to get out of this training; what will help you implement the ideas put forth in this statement, etc.) for the group to read and reflect on before the training begins. (These two mailings could be combined.)

THE LEARNING ENVIRONMENT

- Provide a space that is comfortable and inviting.
- Arrange chairs in a circle in order that each person can see everyone else.
- Appeal to all senses:
  - Utilize newsprint or overheads as often as possible: Catholic social teaching outlines, brainstorming, large group summary discussions, graphics to emphasize points, etc.
  - Write stated expectations from Session 1 on newsprint and post them at each session for participants' own assessment of the training and of themselves.
  - Use symbols where and when possible (e.g., a salt lick and a candle).
  - Display a colorful banner, picture, or other visual element that symbolizes themes, key points, etc.
  - Play soft music as people gather, during prayer, whenever it works.
  - Provide snacks and beverages.
  - Repeat key points from the discussion to summarize both the discussion and the session; highlight those same points in future sessions to tie the whole picture together.
- Provide a book for each participant to help facilitate preparation for, discussion during, and follow-up after each session.
- As much as possible, provide resource handouts that support given discussions (e.g., book and magazine lists, parish models, the USCCB "Communities of Salt and Light" Parish Resource Manual, USCCB resources for each of the seven principles, information on national and local organizations).
- Encourage the use of nametags throughout the training.
- If possible, have at least two facilitators for diversity of style, a change of pace; while one leads the discussion, the other takes notes on newsprint, watches the clocks, pays attention to group dynamics.
- Start on time *and* end on time.

THE TRAINING

- The training is designed to teach as much through process as through content.
- Prayer and community are vital aspects of understanding and incorporating Catholic social teaching into the life of the parish.
- Everything you do during the course of the training reinforces the idea that justice is ultimately about relationships, that our faith is fundamentally social.
- Each session is designed to be three hours long; plan a fifteen minute break about halfway into each session:
  - Suggested times for each "section" are noted in parentheses ( ).
- Prayer
  - Begin and end with prayer; it reinforces our trust and dependence on God for all things. Recite together the *Salt and Light Prayer* (page 3) at the end of Sessions 1–6.
  - Each prayer service is different to model different forms of shared prayer.
  - Readings, intercessions, reflection questions are planned out in each service; common elements such as the call to worship, opening prayer, and song are often left to your discretion to reflect local flavor, current events, and musical library.
- Recap/Overview
  - Maintain a balance here: offer adequate time to hear the wisdom gained while keeping the discussion moving.
  - Ask people about their conversations; try to focus on what was learned, especially about one's self, from the conversation rather than the content (it is not easy to do!), collect people's reflections after discussion.
  - Know your participants. Caution brevity when appropriate. Gently ask for an insight gained when a story starts to meander.
  - Keep the recap *brief*. Bring people from where you were to where you are going in this session.
  - Be sure to state session goals here.

- Small and Large Group Discussion
  - Each appeals more to differing personalities, but both are well received and needed.
  - Encourage people to sit with people they do not know. You may want to maintain the small groups formed in Session 2 throughout the training for continuity; to save time (e.g., limits telling stories); and, to develop a sense of trust and community. On the other hand, group dynamics may dictate that you change the small group make-up periodically.
  - It is absolutely crucial to give clear and concise directions for all small group work; provide as much direction as possible while allowing for group interpretation and creativity.
  - Use newsprint for large group summary discussions; summarize what has been said at the end of each discussion and refer back to the newsprint at the next session.
  - Put any question asked by a participant to the group to solicit their response and generate discussion; summarize key points made; offer your reflections if needed, i.e., if the discussion goes off course.
- Break
  - Provides adequate time for participants to stop, take a breath, take in what they have learned already, informally discuss (or not) what has transpired, chat with an old or new friend, or be quiet.
  - Helps build sense of community
  - Provides facilitator(s) with an opportunity to informally talk with participants and/or address a "problem" situation
- Catholic social teaching (CST)
  - Presented in outline form for easy adaptation; participants like having notes to refer back to later.
  - Use prepared overheads or a flipchart during the presentation (to keep heads from being buried in their notes!).
  - Do not be wedded to the details of the outline; make notes in advance for points you want to make. Much of this is new to people—any point you make is a good one.
  - People will generally retain only one or two points from a session.

- Present with as much interaction and discussion as possible—people respond well; interactive discussion will flow more readily as the training progresses.
- Tie the themes together from session to session; this provides an opportunity to reinforce key points made earlier.
- Evaluation
  - Again, each session is evaluated, and the format for each evaluation differs from session to session for modeling purposes.
  - Evaluation forms are located in the Appendix. Photocopy them to distribute and collect after each session.
  - Do a quick oral check of the group during those sessions which use a written format.
  - Ask participants to quietly reflect on what they have learned today and jot down what it means in relation to their baptismal call.
  - Summarize suggestions from written evaluations at the next session; respond accordingly.
- Preparation for next session
  - Each session requires specific preparation, including some reading and reflection; an interview with someone specifically identified with the session; and completion of the "Styles of Ministry" Quadrants.
  - Participants are asked to think about and jot down the work being done in their parish in the four areas of ministry with regard to the CST principle discussed in each session.
  - Of course, facilitators should encourage participants to read through the chapter to be discussed ahead of time and to pursue any links that might be of interest to them.
- Resources
  - Each session will conclude with a list of resources, including organizations, written materials, videos, and Web sites. The list is not meant to be exhaustive; rather it is a starting point.
  - The facilitator is encouraged to pursue as many of these resources as possible and encourage the participants to pursue them as well.

- At a minimum, draw the participants' attention to these resources after each session.
- Any local resources that can be added to the list are certainly a plus.

THE SESSIONS
SESSION 1: LIFE AND THE DIGNITY OF THE HUMAN PERSON

- Registration: (10 minutes)
  - Begin early; go no longer than 10–15 minutes into the session
  - Participants: sign-in; check the prepared name and address sheet for corrections; pay fee; sign up to bring snacks in groups of three or four for the remaining sessions; and pick up book and name tag
- Prayer: "You are the Salt of the Earth" (p. 12) (30–40 minutes)
  - Quiet, prayerful, self explanatory
  - Provide an overview of the prayer service *before* you begin.
  - Call to Worship—use something people recognize (e.g., "May the peace of our Lord Jesus Christ, the love of God, and the fellowship of the Holy Spirit be with you always." Response: "And also with you.").
  - Pick two readers before the session begins; have the readings marked in a bible or prepared for each reader; keep the quiet reflection between readings to a couple of minutes
  - Closing song suggestions: "This Little Light of Mine," "You Are the Light of the World" from *Godspell*, etc.
- Large Group Discussion: Expectations (10–15 minutes)
  - Brainstorm: What do you hope to get out of this training?
    - List on newsprint; save sheet to be posted during each session
    - Make it clear that the training will not be about a certain stated expectation when appropriate (e.g., how to set boundaries when dealing with the elderly).
  - Review of group and program goals
    - Program goals are stated on p. 13; rather than restating them, refer to the page and make clear the

connection between these goals and the expressed expectations.
- Revisit these goals throughout the training.
- Make a special attempt to challenge folks to think through their own baptismal call throughout the training.
- Course Overview (p. 14) (10–15 minutes)
  - Discussion of expectations leads right into overview of the entire course
  - Keep it clear and concise, and keep it moving!
  - "Styles of Ministry" (p. 16) (10 minutes)
    - Post the prepared graph on newsprint or an overhead; refer to it throughout the remainder of the training.
    - Emphasize that one "does not arrive" at solidarity and thus come to the end of a spiritual journey; rather, each element of social ministry is essential. Each person will find themselves more attracted to or involved with one or another forms of ministry at different points in their lives; and, each of these forms of ministry provides us with different insights into ourselves, others, and God, propelling us on our spiritual journeys (e.g., we can primarily be involved in legislative advocacy, but if we are not in touch with the poor we lose touch with their reality).
    - You will come back to this graph with a different lens in Session 7—that of our own spiritual development (read Albert Nolan's article p. 176).
- Break (10–15 minutes)
- Catholic Social Teaching: General Overview and the Dignity of the Human Person (pp. 19–23) (45–60 minutes)
  - Use overheads or a flip chart.
  - Remember: *Do not* be wedded to the details of the outline; prepare yourself well to walk through the history fairly quickly while highlighting the points that underscore the major theme of the dignity of the human person (e.g., sacredness of life, stewardship, community, etc.)

- As much as you can, make the teaching interactive by asking questions or using the reflection questions.
- Fill in your points with appropriate but brief stories (watch your time!).
- *Reflection* questions are interspersed throughout this outline; if you have the time, use them to generate discussion; otherwise, they can simply stand as they are—questions to reflect on when reviewing the material.
- Discussion questions on human dignity is best done in pairs or groups of three. Give folks 5 minutes to discuss the questions among themselves then briefly open it up for people to share high lights with the large group.
- Shared Prayer (10–15 minutes)
  - Emphasize that this is not a liturgy workshop, but a guide to help plan shared prayer.
  - Mention that not all elements need to be present all of the time
  - Provide sample prayer services (e.g., those used here) or refer to useful resources.
  - You may find that utilizing the large group for the duration of this section will help move the discussion along.
- Baptismal Call
  - Take a few minutes to read the quote provided.
  - Again, the importance of connecting action on behalf of justice to our individual baptisms cannot be overstated.
  - Ask each person to take a minute to reflect quietly on or write about their own baptismal call.
  - Encourage further reflection and refer back to this idea throughout the training.
- Preparation for Session 2: Care for God's Creation (10–15 minutes)
  - Ask participants to read one of the suggested biblical verses and reflect on it somewhere in nature.
  - Encourage people to think of a place beforehand, go there with their bible, pen, and journal pages, and commit themselves to spending 20–25 minutes in this place.
  - People may want to read the verse once, be quiet for 5–10 minutes, and then read it again.

- Encourage participants to use all of their senses—walk them through it: "look with your eyes; what do you see? Close your eyes and listen; what do you hear? Smell? Feel? Make it a sensory experience while allowing the word of God wash over you."
  - Write about the experience.
  - Ask participants to conduct the first of several one-on-one interviews.
  - People may feel affronted at the suggestion that they do not or cannot recognize another's dignity. Offer examples: for some it's a street person who is dirty or jobless or incoherent; for others it is the rich business person who seems to have no compassion; for others it is their nosey next door neighbor, or even a family member.
  - Ask participants to trust the experience; take the leap; talk with the person; and allow themselves to enter fully into the experience.
  - Then, ask them to reflect: what did you learn about yourself? Write it down.
  - Review the "Styles of Ministry" chart. Each session ask participants to think about and jot down the work being done in their parish (or even locally) in the four areas of ministry with regard to the CST principal just discussed. There will be overlap.
- Evaluation (5 minutes)
  - Copy and distribute evaluation (p. 152)
  - As you collect the completed written evaluation forms, ask participants to describe their experience in one word or phrase, going around the circle; it helps build community and energize people
- Closing Prayer
  - After each session, ask participants to stand (hold hands if possible) and recite the Salt and Light Prayer (p. 3) out loud, together.

SESSION 2: CARE FOR GOD'S CREATION

- Opening Prayer (10–15 minutes)
  - Again, open with a familiar opening such as "Peace be with you." Response: "And also with you."
  - Briefly provide overview of the Earth Litany as follows:
    - Part I calls to mind human arrogance and asking forgiveness for the sin of ecological degradation;
    - Part II emphasizes the human role as co-creators with God in restoring the earth community;
    - Part III is a prayer of thanksgiving for all that the earth gives and teaches us.
  - The litany can be read together, or the refrains can be read as a group and the verses read by three pre-chosen readers, or have each verse read by a different person in the circle.
  - Two questions for quiet reflection:
    - Which part of the prayer struck a chord with you?
    - How would you describe your relationship with creation?
  - After a minute or two of silence, invite participants to briefly share an answer to one of the above questions.
  - Close with a song, or a simple Amen.
- Recap/Overview (10–15 minutes)
  - Ask for brief reflections on their prayer experience with nature: How was it? How did you feel? How did the scripture relate to your quiet time?
  - Ask people about their conversations; try to focus on what was learned (especially about one's self) from the conversation rather than the content—it is not easy to do! Collect people's reflection after discussion.
  - Keep the Recap brief. Bring people from where you were to where you are going in this session overview.
- Catholic Social Teaching (50–60 minutes)
  - Again, use visuals; flip charts or overheads
  - There is a lot of material here; cover the highlights

- Section I (p. 32)
  - Allow participants to read it to themselves first. After a few moments, invite them to choose one quote that impresses them most (and have the other explain why).
  - You, too, may highlight the ones that you feel are most important
- Section II, III A (p. 33)
  - While, again, you may want participants to read this section quietly, emphasize John Paul II's role in integrating Care for God's Creation into the realm of Catholic social teaching.
- Section III B & C (p. 35)
  - This is the meat of the outline, giving biblical context and placement in Catholic social teaching.
  - You want to keep this moving while also capturing their attention. This is new to the church, and in this context, likely to the participants
- Break (10–15 minutes)
- Ecological Impact (p. 37) (20–25 minutes)
  - Briefly review the outline with the participants.
  - Ask the participants to quietly complete the Assessment Form
    - Assure them that this is not a test; it will not be collected.
    - Encourage them not to fret over accuracy; their best guess will do.
    - Invite people to reflect quietly (or with a neighbor) on the questions that follow (5 minutes).
  - Open a large group discussion simply by asking people what they learned from the experience.
    - Again, keep focused.
    - You may receive criticism about one or more of the rating questions. If there is a chance to learn about "impact" from the point raised, go with it. If it is a mere quibble, quickly turn it around to make a point about our lifestyles.
- Team Building (p. 42) (25–30 minutes)
  - A way to work through this outline might be to open it up to participants immediately: What comes to mind when you think of team building? How do you do it?

- Use flip charts to jot down their ideas.
- Emphasize big points and add a few that are missing (know your outline well beforehand).
- Summarize with five stages
  - "Re-united" (10 minutes)
    - Form groups of 5 to 7 people
    - Self explanatory
  - Human Knot (5 minutes)
- Preparation for Session 3: Call to Family, Community, and Participation (10–15 minutes)
  - Participants are asked to repeat last week's exercise with nature, choosing the same or a different verse.
  - Ask them to reflect: How was your comfort level this time? Did the 15 minutes go by faster or slower? Were your senses more alert?
  - Participants will be asked to read from the "Communities of Salt and Light" document for each of the remaining sessions.
  - Please note that the page numbers indicated in the manual correspond with those given in the USCCB-produced copy in the back of the latest version of the *Parish Resource Manual*.
  - Remind participants of the reading expectations for each session.
  - Again explain that the preparation includes both *reflection* and *action*, both of which are essential to live out one's faith.
  - *Note*: Obtain the latest version of the document from the USCCB (1-800-235-USCC)
- Evaluation (p. 153) (10 minutes)
  - Before you close, ask participants to take a minute to jot down (in the margins of the book) in their own words what they learned from the session on CST and how it may impact their baptismal calling. Try to do this each session for the major lessons of the day.
  - After participants fill out the written evaluation that you have photocopied, check the pulse of the group by asking for a quick oral reflection (perhaps a one word feeling).
- Closing Prayer: the *Salt and Light* Prayer on page 3 can be used to close each session.

SESSION 3: CALL TO FAMILY, COMMUNITY, AND PARTICIPATION

- Prayer: "Call to Family" (p. 50) (20–30 minutes)
  - Again, choose your readers before the session begins and allow them to read the prayer; choose one or several readers for the litany, depending on the effect you want.
  - Closing song suggestion: Amazing Grace
- Recap/Overview (20 minutes)
  - Invite people to reflect on their time with nature. Ask:
  - How was your comfort level this time? Did the fifteen minutes go by faster or slower? Were your senses more alert? less alert?
  - Summarize findings (positive, negative, changes) from the evaluations
  - Provide a brief "big picture" overview of Sessions 1–3; from personal to interpersonal, etc.
- Explain that two sections from "Communities of Salt and Light" are tied together here; while both are crucial, preaching and education most likely require attention in another arena.
  - Catholic Social Teaching: Call to Family, Community, and Participation (p. 52) (30–40 minutes)
  - Two sections from "Communities of Salt and Light" are separated; a reflection worksheet is presented (p. 53) to help reflect on the message of the "Preaching and Education" section.
  - The discussion on "Family, Work, and Citizenship" is longer and needs to be tied in with the discussion on the dignity of life from Sessions 1 and 2; emphasize the idea that our faith—and therefore salvation— is fundamentally social.
  - Again, *do not* wed yourself to the details; pick your points and emphasize them. Your passion, and *not* details, will capture their attention.
- Break (15 minutes)
- Large and Small Group Work (p. 56) (45–60 minutes)
  - There is a dual purpose for this activity: 1) to increase awareness of the parish as community, and 2) to develop skills

in brainstorming (too often the task of brainstorming results in planning either the first or the most forcefully mentioned idea; groups miss out on the most innovative ideas).

- Thus, while brainstorming in the large group, point out good and bad brainstorming tactics and post the following:
  - *Stay focused* on the topic/issue being discussed (do not stray)
  - *Anything goes*—no holds barred
  - *Push* the ridiculous—to help innovation
  - *Respect* each other's suggestions
  - *Do not analyze* suggestions
  - *No solutions*—do not plan
  - *Use* the fully designated time
- Set a specific time (5 minutes) to brainstorm. When done, summarize the suggestions, probe those that are unclear, and eliminate those that are irrelevant.
- Ask participants to form groups of four to five people *who do not know each other*; this may be their group for the remainder of the course.
- Either choose yourself (saves time and some confusion) or ask each group to pick one of the concerns just mentioned in the large group.
- Each group is asked to *brainstorm* ways in which a parish can act on that concern; ask one person in each group to pay attention to their method of brainstorming (remind people of the posted rules) Give them 5 minutes, and watch the clock. Give them a 1 minute warning.
- Reconvene the large group; ask small groups to identify the concerns they focused on and several of the most creative ideas generated.
- After you hear from all of the groups (keep the discussion moving), go back and ask the large group to reflect on the process of brainstorming: What did and did not work? Were they able to incorporate the brainstorming strategies?
- Preparation for Session 4: Option for the Poor and Vulnerable (p. 57) (10 minutes)

- Ask the participants to read the pertinent section from the bishops' statement and re-read the overview for "Styles of Ministry," (pp. 16-18)
- Place emphasis on this chart—it will be used often throughout the remainder of the training
- Re-emphasize the need to incorporate prayer into parish-related work.
- Again, people are asked to talk to someone new; tie in the social aspect of our faith with the point of these conversations; reinforce their importance by collecting a brief reflection on that which impressed them most significantly from the conversation.
- Evaluation (p. 154): copy, distribute, and collect.
  - Reminder, give participants a minute to summarize what they learned about CST and how it may impact their baptismal calling (in the margins).
  - Sessions 1, 2, 3, and 7 have written evaluations to be collected; again, check the pulse of the group by asking for brief oral feedback. *Note*: This session may end early; it is likely to be your only session with time to spare. If possible, win points and end early!
- Closing Prayer: "Salt and Light", p.3

SESSION 4: OPTION FOR THE POOR AND VULNERABLE
- Prayer: "Blessed are the Poor" (p. 62) (30 minutes)
  - Provide an overview before you begin.
    - Give a brief background on *Populorum Progressio*.
    - Invite everyone to read a paragraph as you go around the circle.
  - Invite reflection at the end of the meditation.
- Catholic Social Teaching: Option for the Poor and the Vulnerable (p. 65) (20–30 minutes)
  - The session overview is delayed until after the segment on CST because this discussion flows naturally from the prayer.
  - This section provides a general overview of the option for the poor, illuminating its biblical and historical roots and its implications.

- Encourage participants to assume a new lens—whichever resonates more clearly with them.
- Again, try to make the session as interactive as possible (i.e., ask the group the header questions: who are the poor?, etc.) and get the *main* points across—leave the details for their own reflection.
- Recap/Overview (10–15 minutes)
  - Follow-up on discussions with an adult or child from your parish; collect reflection papers.
  - Summarize findings from the evaluations; institute the suggested changes that were feasible.
  - Take a few minutes to review their expectations (posted on the wall) and the training goals; are they being met? If not, why not? What can be done to meet those that are feasible?
  - Today's focus: **the elements** of social ministry
    - Still working on interpersonal level, but move from the primary community(ies) to the public arena; greater need to recognize and respect varying perspectives
- Skit and Discussion: "The Door Exercise"[21] (10–15 minutes)

"Where You Stand Depends on Where You Sit"

The purpose of this short play is to help those people who consider their way of seeing things "as the only way things can be." It can help them to understand that their view is coming from where they themselves are in society. It is useful anytime it is needed in the middle of a discussion or it can be used on its own.

This play takes less than one minute to prepare and requires three people. Encourage actors to speak their lines loudly, clearly, and repeatedly, until you end the skit.

Ask two people to sit facing each other, with one person facing the door (if there is more than one door, choose an object in the room of which there is only one, for example the blackboard or the window or the table). This is important. Ask the second person to sit with his or her back to the door. The third person comes to the two of them, from one side, and asks, "Where is the door?" They both respond immediately, the one facing the door says, "In front." The one with his or her back to the door says,

"Behind." This third person asks again, "Where?" and the responses are "In front," "Behind"—each out-shouting the other. The play then ends.

Discussion Questions

1. Who was correct? Was anyone correct for the third person (because the door was at his or her side, not behind or in front)?

2. What does this short play tell us?

3. What parallel does it have to real life?

4. What are the factors that affect our different views of reality?
   a) Culture
   b) Class
   c) Education
   d) Sex, age, etc.

5. What significance can this have for the way we work together as a group?

- "Styles of Ministry" (p. 16) (10 minutes)
  - Review the chart (notes on p.18), discuss the graph, and relate it to the discussion on inter-personal and structural levels, as well as to the discussion on perspective from the skit.
- Break (10 minutes)
- Program Development and Analysis (pp. 68–70) (50–60 minutes)
  - Large Group Discussion on Program Planning
    - This seems to be a difficult process to grasp, largely due to our tendency to have a "solution" and simply hope that the problem fits it.
    - Read through the entire section and know where *you* are going with it.
    - Again, have the outline prepared on a flip chart or over-heads to give people something to follow while you talk.

- Emphasize the need to identify the problem and to break it down to an issue that you can manage *before* you even begin to seek a solution.
- In this session, the small groups will only work through step C: Brainstorming Strategies; thus, when you first present it, only present through step C before they break into small groups; go over the last four steps **briefly** *at the end* of the entire discussion.
- Work through the poverty example as you go.
- Before you break into small groups, you may want to practice breaking problems into issues in the large group (people have a hard time with this concept), e.g., violence broken down to the increase in teen violence on school grounds; and then name the goal).
- Try to avoid a discussion on goals and objectives; at this point, you simply want to focus on a goal (a positive corollary to the identified issue) that names the desired outcome; the brainstormed strategies are different ways to achieve the goal/outcome.
- *Note*: you will come back to this same exercise with a different "problem" next session for practice and greater understanding.
- Small Group Work: Issue Identification and Program Development
  - Make direction very clear; the group is to proceed through step C, Brainstorming Strategies, only
  - Define the problem to be used in small groups and have each group break the given problem down into a winnable issue. (e.g., Problem: One thousand Haitian and Cuban refugees have moved into your parish during the last three months; many are homeless, jobless, hungry in a foreign country without family, friends, or access to resources . . . ; or, use a current/local problem or a problem defined in Session 3's brainstorming session.)
  - Before they break into their groups, reiterate the three main points:

1. Diagnose problem into issue
2. Define goal
3. Brainstorm strategies

- Encourage participants to refer to notes to guide the discussion.
- Check in on groups to answer questions and guide discussion if needed.

- Large Group Summary
  - Summarize group work by listing on newsprint:
    Issue   **Goal**   **Strategies**
  - Offer reflection and guidance as you go (e.g., if suggested strategy does not reflect the stated goal, ask the group how that strategy will meet their goal and guide them to a more appropriate strategy).
  - Once each group has discussed their issue and strategies, summarize the section by restating the main steps and then *briefly* describing the remaining four steps.
- This is an excellent time to provide participants with a list of local support systems that could help parish groups handle the given problem/issue.

- Preparation for Session 5: Rights and Responsibilities (p. 71) (10 minutes)
  - Participants are asked to read the section on Advocacy in "Communities of Salt and Light" as well as "rights" documents (pp. 159–165) with an eye toward their similarities and differences.
  - This session's conversation focuses on someone from the population of their choice; encourage the participants to talk with the person as an equal, not as a potential "client," thereby avoiding a client/adviser relationship.

- Evaluation (p. 155) (10 minutes)
  - *Reminder*: give participants a minute to summarize (in writing) an insight to their own baptismal call as a result of today's session.
  - The purpose of this evaluation is to focus on *the process* of the training.

- Seek input on or ask a few of the questions; *always* allow the group to provide input on a question before you make any comments.
- Here is an excellent opportunity to challenge the participants to think through the effect this process has had on them, especially in light of their baptismal call.
- Mention that each person will be expected to articulate a few specific goals as a result of this training (i.e., Personal Action Plan, Session 7).

SESSION 5: RIGHTS AND RESPONSIBILITIES
- Prayer: "Going Upstream" (p. 76) (20–30 minutes)
- Call to Worship: Invoke the Trinity
  - Invite someone to read the parable; you may want to get three readers—a narrator (normal text), the "lone voice," and the elders.
  - Use the discussion structure provided on p. 135 for the skit, "Where You Stand Depends on Where You Sit."
    - **Description:** What is going on here? (**X**)
    - **First Analysis:** Why is **X** happening?
    - **Real Life:** Does **X** happen in real life?
    - **Related Problems**: What problem does **X** lead to?
    - **Root Causes:** What are the root causes of **X** problems?
    - **Action Planning:** What can we do about it? *(Note: fill **X** in with the problems discussed by the group.)*
  - Try to maintain a spiritual tone rather than an intellectual one—a challenge!
- Recap/Overview (10 minutes)
  - Ask about the conversations, focusing on the insights gained, not the details of the conversation; collect reflections.
  - Review today's agenda: note that we are moving into the structural level of reality.
    - Refer to the graph of the quadrants, place today's discussion within the given model, and introduce the idea of structures and systems within that context (i.e., advocacy)

- Connect today's discussion with the point, "Where you stand depends on where you sit." (e.g., who is speaking for whom?)
- Catholic Social Teaching: Rights and Responsibilities (p. 77) (10–15 minutes)
  - Note: the U.S. has not ratified the UN Declaration; call the UN for exact figures on which countries have currently ratified the Declaration.
  - Key points: increased recognition of basic human rights with each document; *Pacem in Terris* is the only one that balances the rights with responsibilities (explain).
  - As always, try to draw out these points through discussion (as opposed to lecture), then summarize at the end.
- Introduction to the structural response to social issues (Section II, p. 77) (15–20 minutes)
  - The above leads right into this discussion.
  - Again, provide some context: mention your earlier focus on the personal and interpersonal levels of reality/relationships and introduce the structural level with an example (e.g., health care reform is likely to affect Aunt Ann).
  - Either offer or ask for examples for each line you choose to discuss (e.g., victim—an abused child; cause—domestic violence); the point to get across is that operating on the personal/interpersonal level of reality involves different relationships, skills and focus than those involved at the structural level.
- Large Group Discussion: Advocacy (15–20 minutes)
  - Discuss: What is it? Why is it necessary? How does it relate to human rights and responsibilities?
  - Take notes on newsprint; summarize the first three questions before you start to brainstorm the last one.
  - Brainstorm: How do we do it?
- Summary
  - Wrap the whole discussion up by referring to the graphic (p. 78) and allow the group (or you) to offer a reflection of the points just made.
- Break (15 minutes)

- Small Group Work: Program Development (p. 79) (35–40 minutes)
  - Review the steps introduced in Session 4 (p. 68) in *large group*; go over any "trouble spots," where there seemed to be a lack of understanding last session.
  - Break into the same small groups as the last time.
  - Offer the same problem, only now the issue must provoke the group/parish to "go up the river," (e.g., the goal must be geared toward a structural response and strategies to reflect systemic change).
  - Depending on how well this process went in Session 4, you may want to encourage groups to begin to analyze the feasibility of each strategy; make sure they have the first three steps down first.
  - Check in on groups and help them focus their discussion where necessary (many people find it hard to think in terms of a structural response; we find some groups mostly debating whether a given idea is indeed structural).
- Large Group Summary (20–25 minutes)
  - Again, have group summarize work:

Issue	Goal	Strategy Analysis

  - *Briefly* review remaining steps (and perhaps, suggest that this may be a topic for a more in depth workshop at a given parish).
- Preparation for Session 6: The Dignity of Work and the Rights of Workers (10 minutes)
  - Emphasize the importance of meeting with the pastor and or staff to *listen* to his or her ideas and interests in the social mission; encourage participants to demonstrate interest and build collaboration.
  - At this point, it will be clear whether people are conducting the conversations; if the majority are not, encourage them to set up an appointment with their pastor at some point in the near future if not for the training, for the sake of their own work in and relationship to their parish.
- Oral Evaluation (10 minutes)
  - Reminder: allow the participants time to summarize for themselves what they have learned and how it may impact their baptismal call.

- Three questions/three columns:

  What worked?   **What didn't**   **How would you change it?**
- For any negative criticism, ask for a possible, positive alternative.
- Closing Prayer

SESSION 6: THE DIGNITY OF WORK AND THE RIGHTS OF WORKERS

- Opening Prayer (5 minutes)
  - Because a significant amount of time is devoted to scriptural reflection, a brief, yet pertinent, opening prayer should be offered here.
  - Suggestion: inspirational prayer, reading, or song
- Recap/Overview (10 minutes)
  - Ask about conversations with pastors or staff; collect reflections, again focusing on insights, not details.
  - Explain today's agenda; again, refer to the graph of the quadrants—place the discussion.
- Catholic Social Teaching: "The Dignity of Work and the Rights of Workers" (p. 84) (10 minutes)
  - Self explanatory and not too long
  - Emphasize subsidiarity; leads into next discussion
    - Ask participants to read the definition quietly while one person reads it aloud.
    - Ask: What does this mean to you? Can you think of an example?
    - Summarize with a succinct definition.
- Scriptural Basis for Community Organizing (p. 85) (60 minutes)
  - Have the scripture readings pre-printed and distributed to the readers, if not everyone.
  - Ask people to put their books away in order to listen and reflect on the readings.
  - After each reading, ask the group what is going on here; what is Jesus trying to say?
  - You may want to group the last four readings and extract the main points for the sake of time.

- While the outline is your guide, the discussion can go any where and much is left to the Holy Spirit; allow that to happen (for that is what makes this so exciting!).
- The idea, of course, is to get across the idea that Jesus truly is the model "organizer".
- Use newsprint to emphasize key points
- Congregation-Based Organizing (p. 88) (15 minutes)
  - Refer people to the outline for their own reflections. Do not review it now, as it is too much to absorb.
  - Draw parallels between Jesus' methods and modern day organizing.
  - Emphasize that organizing provides both an avenue for community work (cite local congregation-based organizing efforts) *and* a method for group development; explain.
- Break (10 minutes)
- Skill Development: Volunteer Recruitment and One-on-One Interviews (p. 89) (45–50 minutes)
  - Volunteer recruitment seems to be a primary concern for people.
  - Distinguish between two purposes: recruitment for a given program; and an invitation to fulfill one's baptismal call through the social mission of the church—both are necessary.
  - In the large group:
    - Brainstorm recruiting tactics.
    - Briefly review and solicit (concise) suggestions for more successful attempts of the traditional recruiting methods.
    - Allow the group to identify the most effective method— one-on-one meetings.
    - Facilitate a large group discussion on what that meeting might look like; again, make it clear that recruitment purpose drives the style of the meeting.
  - Model an interview by allowing the group to ask you (or some-one in the group) questions as if on an interview; stop after 5–10 minutes and critique the process.
  - If time permits, allow the group to practice in pairs.
  - Suggest that each parish form a committee whose sole responsibility is to interview parishioners to identify new leaders and listen to people's concerns.

- Be sure to refer to the handouts (pp. 89-93) (suggest that this may be another topic for a parish workshop).
- Preparation for Session 7: Solidarity (p. 93) (10 minutes)
  - Emphasize the importance of the Albert Nolan article: "The Service to the Poor and Spiritual Growth" (p. 176).
  - Re-introduce the Parish Assessment and Personal Action Plan (p. 184); ask participants to complete sections A and B and begin D *prior* to the next session (there will be time to complete section C, during the next session).
    - You will need to walk through this form with participants; present it as a summary of the training and a means to help them take what has been learned and put it into action.
    - Discuss its purpose: a tool for assessing and helping to prioritize the needs of the parish and the interests and abilities of the individual (especially with regard to time).
    - Emphasize confidentiality.
    - Explain your procedure: make a copy and return the original to the person; keep a copy on file and send it to the respective person about 6–9 months after the end of the course.
    - The form is designed for you to learn the level of involvement and the areas of interest in which the individual and the parish wish your office to participate; keep records accordingly.
- Oral Evaluation (10 minutes)
  - *Reminder*: give participants a minute to summarize their learnings and reflect on how it may impact their baptismal call.
  - Use a similar format as last time or some other known process.
- Closing Prayer

SESSION 7: SOLIDARITY
- Opening Prayer (5 minutes)
  - The prayer service will close the session and the training; simply open with a brief and pertinent prayer (e.g., "The Road Ahead" by Thomas Merton).

- Recap/Overview (15 minutes)
  - Seek comments on Albert Nolan's article; this is an excellent starting point for today's discussion.
  - Walk through the graph of the quadrants with an eye to the spiritual growth described by Nolan.
  - Tie in reflections with training overview and today's agenda
- Catholic Social Teaching: Solidarity (p. 98) (30 minutes)
  - Convey the progression of Catholic social teaching over the last 100+ years, the urgency of the teachings, and the centrality of solidarity in that thought.
  - Allow for ample reflection and discussion.
  - Relate discussion to current events.
  - Again, let go of details and go for the "spirit" of the message; try to facilitate a discussion rather than give a strict lecture.
  - Here might be a good place to use a video, bring in a guest speaker, etc.
- Skill Development: Leadership (p. 101) (20 minutes)
  - Ask the large group to brainstorm leadership qualities; then compare the generated list with that provided (p. 101).
    - Ask people to quietly reflect on which of those qualities they possess.
  - You may want to lay out different leadership styles (e.g., those described in Myers-Briggs language) and ask participants to identify their own preferred style of leadership: the key here is to help individuals see themselves as leaders, perhaps with a style different from the stereotypical "leader."
  - Use the above discussion to aid in the completion of the Personal Action Plan (p. 184).
    - Participants will have completed sections A, B, and most of D. Having given some introduction to section C, give time for participants to complete the form; collect them and return the originals to each person as soon as you have made copies for the file.
- Break (15 minutes)

- Skill Development: Facilitation and Effective Meetings (p. 103) (60 minutes)
  - Small Group Exercise: "How to Run a Meeting"
    - Three (or four) small groups (use either established groups or ask for volunteers) are asked to role play a meeting, one group at a time with the other groups watching.
    - In all but the last role play, each person is given a role pre-determined by the trainer (e.g., people draw roles from a hat, including at least one "trouble personality": gossip, silent worker, class clown; and "gatekeeper"—the unofficial person with whom all ideas must pass).
    - For the first role play, players should receive little to no direction as far as agenda and facilitator are concerned; have some definite "trouble personalities" in the group; let them go at it for about 5 minutes.
    - Each successive group (1–2 more) should have at least a designated facilitator and increasingly clearer agendas while some "trouble personalities" remain (i.e., each role play ideally should be an improvement in meeting format over the previous one).
    - Give each group a decision to make, generally the same one (hence, the reason for meeting): e.g., pick the name for your group; choose the fund raising event that your group will host this year, etc.
  - Small groups will perform each role play for the large group.
  - After each role play, the entire group is to evaluate the meeting; what worked, what didn't; were there any problems, and if so, what was the source; how did the group deal with problems; was their method effective; what are other effective ways to deal with that situation.
    - Direct some questions directly to the players (e.g., how did it feel when. . . ?).
    - Write notes on newsprint; summarize major learnings at the end.

- Time will generally allow two to three role plays; the last role play ideally should model a "good meeting:" participants play themselves with a designated facilitator, record keeper, and clear agenda, and they model what has been learned.
- Summarize the exercise with five or six key points about effective meetings (p. 106).
- Evaluation: Written and Oral (pp. 157–158) (15 minutes)
  - Take some time to do an oral evaluation (i.e., Good? Bad? Changes?) of the session and of the overall training, after people complete the written form.
  - Encourage people to complete the Solidarity Quadrants.
- Closing Prayer Service: "Living and Dying in Solidarity" (p. 108).
  - Give an overview before you begin.
  - Arrange for readers before the prayer.
  - Have tapers in front of each person designated to read one of the quotes from the four women; before she or he reads the quote, have him or her light the candle as a symbol of solidarity.
  - Once again we are reminded of our baptismal call. Tie this to the reflection questions. Remind participants that these four women did not set out to die as part of their "call." They followed the Lord in little ways, like going to the airport to welcome fellow missionaries—a Christian action that resulted in their death. What are some of the little ways people have grown or changed (i.e., "heard the call"). Invite folks to bring that call to prayer, perhaps try helping them to ritualize it.
  - Ask everyone to raise their hand and read the blessing together.

SESSION 8: FORMING A COMMUNITY OF SALT AND LIGHT: FOLLOW-UP MEETING
- If more than two weeks after the last session, a pre-meeting letter should be sent to all participants and include:
  - Agenda
  - Twenty Key Ideas
  - Class specific set of "Training Expectations" from Session 1

- The following reflection questions: *Which quote or idea strikes you the most and why? How is it relevant to what you would like to see continue from the* Salt and Light *course?*
- Invite people to gather fifteen minutes before the meeting is scheduled to begin.
  - Continue with a similar set-up as used during the training.
  - Make sure refreshments are provided.
- Opening prayer (30 minutes depending on number of people)
  - Include a reflection on the "Twenty Key Ideas."
  - Reflect on the questions from the pre-meeting letter.
- Our expectations rating sheet (30 minutes)
  - Facilitators will need to create a different rating sheet based on the "our expectations" brainstorm of Session 1 for each class.
  - The handout should include a rating scale to aid the participants' evaluations of the course with regard to their own expectations.
  - The sheet allows participants to evaluate their own progress based on the goals they came up with as a group.
  - The sheet should be given to participants at the end of the last session, or in a follow-up mailing. It can be used to encourage a follow-up meeting if there is not one determined at the last session.
  - The facilitator should bring a few extra copies in case participants forget them.
  - *Note*: A newsprint visual can be created for each goal, taped to the walls, where participants walk around and indicate their ratings. This can be done as they initially arrive, asking them to indicate their ratings before taking a seat. The facilitator can then tally the ratings to get an average for a *group* rating (bring a calculator). This might help focus the discussion, particularly for weak areas as well as for successes.
  - Briefly focus (about 5 minutes each) large group discussion time on "goals we met" and "didn't meet," allowing the rest of the time to brainstorm and discuss "goals for the future."

Program Development (30 minutes)
- Small groups consider the brainstormed goals for the future (15 minutes), picking one and applying the program development (Sessions 4 and 5) model to their discussion.
- A Program Development Worksheet is provided with the session materials.
- Large group gathers for further discussion/consensus (15 minutes).
- If the group is small enough, this could be done as a large group discussion for the entire half hour.

- Next Steps/Action (25 minutes)
  - *Option one*: Continue to explore CST themes through various additional activities from outside resources:
    - urban or rural plunges
    - a "Journey to Justice" retreat
    - participating in the "JustFaith" nine month formation course
    - creating a Parish Social Ministry committee or team (if non-existent)
    - other
  - *Option two*: Bring copies of "A Personal Action Plan" for further analysis. They could choose to do this with additional members of the parish or just themselves. Encourage a fuller analysis of how the parish is incorporating CST into parish life by inviting parish leaders and staff, parish committees, and work-groups to complete this tool. Such analysis may involve several more meetings.
  - These tools could be completed individually and then in small groups. More minds working together may get a fuller picture of what is happening in the parish as well as invigorate imagination/brainstorming of what could be done.
  - Under each CST theme, the small group notes two successes, two challenges (area needing improvement), and one or two recommendations for future planning or parish action.
    - These successes, challenges, and recommendations are brought back to the large group for dialogue and discussion and planning for parish action.

- Then the "Program Planning—Strategy Development" skills are put into place (Sessions 3 and 4 worksheets).
- *Option three:* Continue with Program Development of one, two, or all three of their winnable issues (from Sessions 4 and 5).
  - Proceed slowly; continued strategy analysis may be needed before going forward any further with the program development.
- *Option four:* If none of the above options fit into the follow-up needs based on group discussions, then some basic "next step" work needs to occur:
  - what will we do?
  - when will we do it?
  - what resources do we need?
  - who will plan and coordinate?
- Concluding Prayer: "Salt and Light" Prayer, p. 3

APPENDIX

EVALUATION
SESSION 1: LIFE AND THE DIGNITY OF THE HUMAN PERSON

Overall, how would you describe this session, using one word or phrase? _____

_____

How effective were each of the following?

facilitators _____

accommodations _____

_____

program content, materials _____

_____

program process, discussion, etc._____

_____

your participation (realizing that much of what you get out of this course is dependent upon what you put into it) _____

_____

Did anything unusual or significant happen either for you or the group that stands out in your mind—tensions, breakthroughs, connections, etc.? _____

_____

_____

Did you learn anything new today? What was it? _____

_____

Other comments _____

_____

Name (optional) _____ **Date** _____

EVALUATION
SESSION 2: CARE FOR GOD'S CREATION

Overall, how would you describe this session, using one word or phrase? _____

_____

What image or idea struck you from the session? _____

_____

_____

_____

Has your idea of "right relationship" with God's creation been affected by what we discussed? Why or why not?

_____

_____

_____

_____

_____

Which was your favorite part of this session and why? _____

_____

_____

_____

_____

Which was your least favorite part of this session and why? _____

_____

_____

_____

_____

Name (optional) _____ **Date** _____

EVALUATION
SESSION 3: CALL TO FAMILY, COMMUNITY, AND PARTICIPATION

How would you rate: (Please circle)	Poor	Fair	Good	Very Good	Excellent
this session, overall	1	2	3	4	5
opening prayer	1	2	3	4	5
teaching on Family, Community, and Participation	1	2	3	4	5
large group discussion	1	2	3	4	5
small group work on community	1	2	3	4	5
large group discussion of programs	1	2	3	4	5
your own performance	1	2	3	4	5
the "homework"—between session activities/readings	1	2	3	4	5

Comment on one positive and one negative thing from today that sticks out in your mind:

_____

_____

What group development processes (e.g., brainstorming, small or large group discussion, etc.) would you like to incorporate in your work with the parish? When and why?

_____

_____

Other comments _____

_____

Name (optional) _____ **Date** _____

154   BECOMING A COMMUNITY OF SALT AND LIGHT

EVALUATION
SESSION 4:
OPTION FOR THE POOR AND VULNERABLE
WHY DO WE DO WHAT WE DO?[23]

1. Why do we have introductions at the beginning of the training?

2. Why do we ask people to introduce a partner rather than introducing themselves?

3. Why do we ask participants what they expect of the training?

4. Why do we ask people to discuss in groups of three?

5. Why do we ask people to discuss in groups of five or six rather than groups of three?

6. Why do we invite participants to come in parish teams rather than as isolated individuals?

7. Why do we ask people to find people they do not know well at the beginning of a workshop to discuss topics?

8. Why do we put the chairs in a circle?

9. Why do we brainstorm some topics and not others?

10. Why might we stop some discussions and have people form a "buzz group" to talk with his or her neighbor?

11. Why do we come back to the large group after small group work and debrief?

12. Why do we use newsprint? When is it helpful and when is it not helpful to use newsprint?

13. Why do we use diagrams, skits, stories, etc.?

14. Why do we have discussions on the poor and the oppressed in our society?

15. Why do we have discussions on the influence of the economically well off in our society?

16. Why do we have participants evaluate the training? Why is this important especially at the middle and at the end of the course?

17. Why do we ask you to talk with someone new to you after each session?

18. Why do we ask you what you learned about yourself from those conversations?

SELF EVALUATION: HOW DOES WHAT WE DO AFFECT YOU?

1. What about the training has had the most significant impact on you thus far, positive or negative?

2. What will you bring back to your work in the parish?

3. In Baptism each of us is called to discipleship. What path are you being called to follow?

FINAL EVALUATION

1. Overall, how would you describe the training, using *one* word or phrase?

_____

_____

2. How would you rate the effectiveness of the following, on a scale from 1 (poor) to 5 (excellent); please comment on anything rated a three or lower.

Comments

_____ Catholic Social Teaching _____

_____ Overview of Parish Social Ministry _____

_____ Development of Elements of the Social Mission: outreach; advocacy; organizing; solidarity

_____

_____

_____ Skill Development: Program development; recruitment; leadership development; facilitation

_____

_____

_____ Materials _____

_____ Assignments _____

_____ Session Structure _____

_____ Overall Group Participation and Interaction _____

_____ Small Group Work _____

_____ Large Group Work _____

_____ Prayer and Reflection _____

_____ Facilitation _____

_____ Your Own Participation _____

_____ Other _____

Additional Comments: _____

3. Name *one* new thing that you learned from this course in terms of:

Content: _____

_____

Process: _____

_____

Skill Development: _____

_____

4. Name *one* thing that you had hoped to learn but didn't, in terms of:

Content: _____

_____

Process: _____

_____

_____

Skill Development: _____

_____

5. Which session was most beneficial to you and why? _____

_____

_____

6. Which session was least beneficial to you and why? _____

_____

_____

7. How applicable is this training to parish groups? _____

Why? _____

What would you do/change to make this a more effective training program for parish lay leaders?

_____

Name (optional) _____ **Date** _____

Amendments to the U.S. Constitution, "The Bill of Rights"

Article [I.]

Congress shall make no law respecting an establishment of religion, or prohibiting the free exercise thereof; or abridging the freedom of speech, or of the press; or the right of the people peaceably to assemble, and to petition the Government for a redress of grievances.

Article [II.]

A well regulated Militia, being necessary to the security of a free State, the right of the people to keep and bear Arms, shall not be infringed.

Article [III.]

No Soldier shall, in time of peace be quartered in any house, without the consent of the Owner, nor in time of war, but in a manner to be prescribed by law.

Article [IV.]

The right of the people to be secure in their persons, houses, papers, and effects, against unreasonable searches and seizures, shall not be violated, and no Warrants shall issue, but upon probable cause, supported by Oath or affirmation, and particularly describing the place to be searched, and the persons or things to be seized.

Article [V.]

No person shall be held to answer for a capital, or otherwise infamous crime, unless on a presentment or indictment of a Grand Jury, except in cases arising in the land or naval forces, or in the Militia, when in actual service in time of War or public danger; nor shall any person be subject for the same offence to be twice put in jeopardy of life or limb; nor shall be compelled in any criminal case to be a witness against himself, nor be deprived of life, liberty, or property, without due process of law; nor shall private property be taken for public use, without just compensation.

Article [VI.]

In all criminal prosecutions, the accused shall enjoy the right to a speedy and public trial, by an impartial jury of the State and district wherein the crime shall have been committed, which district shall have been previously ascertained by law, and to be informed of the nature and cause of the accusation; to be confronted with the witnesses against him; to have compulsory process for obtaining witnesses in his favor, and to have the Assistance of Counsel for his defense.

Article [VII.]

In Suits at common law, where the value in controversy shall exceed twenty dollars, the right of trial by jury shall be preserved, and no fact tried by a jury, shall be otherwise re-examined in any Court of the United States, than according to the rules of the common law.

Article [VIII.]

Excessive bail shall not be required, nor excessive fines imposed, nor cruel and unusual punishments inflicted.

Article [IX.]

The enumeration in the Constitution, of certain rights, shall not be construed to deny or disparage others retained by the people.

Article [X.]

The powers not delegated to the United States by the Constitution, nor prohibited by it to the States, are reserved to the States respectively, or to the people.

UNIVERSAL DECLARATION OF HUMAN RIGHTS

Adopted and proclaimed by General Assembly resolution 217 A (III) of 10 December 1948

On December 10, 1948, the General Assembly of the United Nations adopted and proclaimed the Universal Declaration of Human Rights, the full text of which appears in the following pages. Following this historic act the Assembly called upon all Member countries to publicize the text of the Declaration and "to cause it to be disseminated, displayed, read and expounded principally in schools and other educational institutions, without distinction based on the political status of countries or territories."

Preamble

Whereas recognition of the inherent dignity and of the equal and inalienable rights of all members of the human family is the foundation of freedom, justice and peace in the world,

Whereas disregard and contempt for human rights have resulted in barbarous acts which have outraged the conscience of mankind, and the advent of a world in which human beings shall enjoy freedom of speech and belief and freedom from fear and want has been proclaimed as the highest aspiration of the common people,

Whereas it is essential, if man is not to be compelled to have recourse, as a last resort, to rebellion against tyranny and oppression, that human rights should be protected by the rule of law,

Whereas it is essential to promote the development of friendly relations between nations,

Whereas the peoples of the United Nations have in the Charter reaffirmed their faith in fundamental human rights, in the dignity and worth of the human person and in the equal rights of men and women and have determined to promote social progress and better standards of life in larger freedom,

Whereas Member States have pledged themselves to achieve, in co-operation with the United Nations, the promotion of universal respect for and observance of human rights and fundamental freedoms,

Whereas a common understanding of these rights and freedoms is of the greatest importance for the full realization of this pledge,

Now, Therefore *The General Assembly* proclaims this *Universal Declaration of Human Rights* as a common standard of achievement for all peoples and all nations, to the end that every individual and every organ of society, keeping this Declaration constantly in mind, shall strive by teaching and education to promote respect for these rights and freedoms and by progressive measures, national and international, to secure their universal and effective recognition and observance, both among the peoples of Member States themselves and among the peoples of territories under their jurisdiction.

Article 1.

All human beings are born free and equal in dignity and rights. They are endowed with reason and conscience and should act towards one another in a spirit of brotherhood.

Article 2.

Everyone is entitled to all the rights and freedoms set forth in this Declaration, without distinction of any kind, such as race, color, sex, language, religion, political or other opinion, national or social origin, property, birth or other status. Furthermore, no distinction shall be made on the basis of the political, jurisdictional or international status of the country or territory to which a person belongs, whether it be independent, trust, non-self-governing or under any other limitation of sovereignty.

Article 3.

Everyone has the right to life, liberty and security of person.

Article 4.

No one shall be held in slavery or servitude; slavery and the slave trade shall be prohibited in all their forms.

Article 5.

No one shall be subjected to torture or to cruel, inhuman or degrading treatment or punishment.

Article 6.

Everyone has the right to recognition everywhere as a person before the law.

Article 7.

All are equal before the law and are entitled without any discrimination to equal protection of the law. All are entitled to equal protection against any discrimination in violation of this Declaration and against any incitement to such discrimination.

Article 8.

Everyone has the right to an effective remedy by the competent national tribunals for acts violating the fundamental rights granted him by the constitution or by law.

Article 9.

No one shall be subjected to arbitrary arrest, detention or exile.

Article 10.

Everyone is entitled in full equality to a fair and public hearing by an independent and impartial tribunal, in the determination of his rights and obligations and of any criminal charge against him.

Article 11.

(1) Everyone charged with a penal offense has the right to be presumed innocent until proved guilty according to law in a public trial at which he has had all the guarantees necessary for his defense.

(2) No one shall be held guilty of any penal offense on account of any act or omission which did not constitute a penal offense, under national or international law, at the time when it was committed. Nor shall a heavier penalty be imposed than the one that was applicable at the time the penal offense was committed.

Article 12.

No one shall be subjected to arbitrary interference with his privacy, family, home or correspondence, nor to attacks upon his honor and reputation. Everyone has the right to the protection of the law against such interference or attacks.

Article 13.

(1) Everyone has the right to freedom of movement and residence within the borders of each state.

(2) Everyone has the right to leave any country, including his own, and to return to his country.

Article 14.

(1) Everyone has the right to seek and to enjoy in other countries asylum from persecution.

(2) This right may not be invoked in the case of prosecutions genuinely arising from non-political crimes or from acts contrary to the purposes and principles of the United Nations.

Article 15.

(1) Everyone has the right to a nationality.

(2) No one shall be arbitrarily deprived of his nationality nor denied the right to change his nationality.

Article 16.

(1) Men and women of full age, without any limitation due to race, nationality or religion, have the right to marry and to found a family. They are entitled to equal rights as to marriage, during marriage and at its dissolution.

(2) Marriage shall be entered into only with the free and full consent of the intending spouses.

(3) The family is the natural and fundamental group unit of society and is entitled to protection by society and the State.

Article 17.

(1) Everyone has the right to own property alone as well as in association with others.

(2) No one shall be arbitrarily deprived of his property.

Article 18.

Everyone has the right to freedom of thought, conscience and religion; this right includes freedom to change his religion or belief, and freedom, either alone or in community with others and in public or private, to manifest his religion or belief in teaching, practice, worship and observance.

Article 19.

Everyone has the right to freedom of opinion and expression; this right includes freedom to hold opinions without interference and to seek, receive and impart information and ideas through any media and regardless of frontiers.

Article 20.

(1) Everyone has the right to freedom of peaceful assembly and association.

(2) No one may be compelled to belong to an association.

Article 21.

(1) Everyone has the right to take part in the government of his country, directly or through freely chosen representatives.

(2) Everyone has the right of equal access to public service in his country.

(3) The will of the people shall be the basis of the authority of government; this will shall be expressed in periodic and genuine elections which shall be by universal and equal suffrage and shall be held by secret vote or by equivalent free voting procedures.

Article 22.

Everyone, as a member of society, has the right to social security and is entitled to realization, through national effort and international co-operation and in accordance with the organization and resources of each State, of the economic, social and cultural rights indispensable for his dignity and the free development of his personality.

Article 23.

(1) Everyone has the right to work, to free choice of employment, to just and favorable conditions of work and to protection against unemployment.

(2) Everyone, without any discrimination, has the right to equal pay for equal work.

(3) Everyone who works has the right to just and favorable remuneration ensuring for himself and his family an existence worthy of human dignity, and supplemented, if necessary, by other means of social protection.

(4) Everyone has the right to form and to join trade unions for the protection of his interests.

Article 24.

Everyone has the right to rest and leisure, including reasonable limitation of working hours and periodic holidays with pay.

Article 25.

(1) Everyone has the right to a standard of living adequate for the health and well-being of himself and of his family, including food, clothing, housing and medical care and necessary social services, and the right to security in the event of unemployment, sickness, disability, widowhood, old age or other lack of livelihood in circumstances beyond his control.

(2) Motherhood and childhood are entitled to special care and assistance. All children, whether born in or out of wedlock, shall enjoy the same social protection.

Article 26.

(1) Everyone has the right to education. Education shall be free, at least in the elementary and fundamental stages. Elementary education shall be

compulsory. Technical and professional education shall be made generally available and higher education shall be equally accessible to all on the basis of merit.

(2) Education shall be directed to the full development of the human personality and to the strengthening of respect for human rights and fundamental freedoms. It shall promote understanding, tolerance and friendship among all nations, racial or religious groups, and shall further the activities of the United Nations for the maintenance of peace.

(3) Parents have a prior right to choose the kind of education that shall be given to their children.

Article 27.

(1) Everyone has the right freely to participate in the cultural life of the community, to enjoy the arts and to share in scientific advancement and its benefits.

(2) Everyone has the right to the protection of the moral and material interests resulting from any scientific, literary or artistic production of which he is the author.

Article 28.

Everyone is entitled to a social and international order in which the rights and freedoms set forth in this Declaration can be fully realized.

EXCERPTED FROM *PACEM IN TERRIS*
POPE JOHN XXIII, APRIL 11, 1963

Rights

11. [T]he right to live. He has the right to bodily integrity . . . the means necessary for the proper development of life, particularly food, clothing, shelter, medical care, rest, and . . . the necessary social services.
12. [R]ight to be respected . . . a right to his good name . . . a right to freedom in investigating the truth . . . to freedom of speech and publication . . . to freedom to pursue whatever profession he may choose.
13. [T]o share in the benefits of culture . . . to receive a good general education, and a technical or professional training consistent with the degree of educational development in his own country.
14. [T]o worship God in accordance with the right dictates of his own conscience, and to profess his religion both in private and in public.

15. [T]he right to choose . . . the kind of life which appeals to him: whether it is to found a family or to embrace the priesthood or the religious life.
16. The family, founded upon marriage freely contracted, one and indissoluble, must be regarded as the natural, primary cell of human society.
17. [T]he support and education of children is a right which belongs primarily to the parents.
18. [T]he inherent right not only to be given the opportunity to work, but also to be allowed the exercise of personal initiative in the work he does.
19. The conditions in which a man works form a necessary corollary to these rights. They must not . . . weaken his physical or moral fibre, or militate against the proper development of adolescence to adulthood.
20. [T]he right to engage in economic activities suited to his degree of responsibility. . . . The amount a worker receives must be sufficient . . . to allow him and his family a standard of living consistent with human dignity.
21. [T]he right to the private ownership of property, including that of productive goods.
22. [T]he right to own private property entails a social obligation as well.
23. [T]he right to meet together and to form associations with his fellows.
25. [T]he right to freedom of movement and of residence.
26. [R]ight to take an active part in public life, and to make his own contribution to the common welfare.
27. [H]e is entitled to the legal protection of his rights, and such protection must be effective, unbiased, and strictly just.

Duties
28. The natural rights . . . are inextricably bound up with as many duties, . . . [and] derive their origin, sustenance, and indestructibility from the natural law, which in conferring the one imposes the other.
29. [T]he right to live involves the duty to preserve one's life; the right to a decent standard of living, the duty to live in a becoming fashion; the right to be free to seek out the truth, the duty to devote oneself to an ever deeper and wider search for it.
30. Once this is admitted, it follows that in human society one man's natural right gives rise to a corresponding duty in other men; the duty, that is, of recognizing and respecting that right.
31. [T]hey must live together and consult each other's interests. That men should recognize and perform their respective rights and duties is imperative to a well-ordered society.

32. [I]t is useless to admit that a man has a right to the necessities of life, unless we also do all in our power to supply him with means sufficient for his livelihood.
33. [S]ociety must not only be well ordered, it must also provide men with abundant resources. This postulates . . . the involvement and collaboration of all men.
34. Man's personal dignity requires . . . that he enjoy freedom and be able to make up his own mind when he acts. [H]is association with his fellows . . . should be primarily a matter of his own personal decision.
35. [B]efore a society can be considered well ordered, creative, and consonant with human dignity, it must be based on truth. . . . Human society demands that men be guided by justice, respect the rights of others and do their duty . . . [and] with reason, assume responsibility for their own actions.

An Introduction To Church-Based Organizing
What Is Church-Based Organizing?

The Goal

In one sense the goal of church-based organizing is no different from that of any other kind of organizing. People organize to have power over the many decisions that affect their lives. Organizers have always sought to enable workers or neighbors to get what they need to live their lives in relative peace and happiness. Labor organizes to achieve just wages, health care, pensions, vacation time, and reasonable hours. Parents organize to improve the schools their children attend, the parks in which their children play, and the health care facilities in the community. Neighbors organize to reduce crime, get rid of the cockroaches and rodents, improve garbage collection, fight higher taxes, and too often, to keep a halfway house for addicts out of their neighborhood.

Similarly, church-based organizing is about empowering people to achieve the goals they have for themselves, their families, their communities, and also for their parishes. The principal difference is that the church approaches organizing with a particular set of religious values, social teachings, and beliefs. Its basic building block for organizing is the congregation or parish.

It is interesting that, while business and political leaders have long tended to see power there, congregations and parishes usually do not think of themselves as having much power. In fact, they have significant power. The primary components of power are numbers of people, money, and commitment. Most local churches have all three, a fact that has not been missed by organizers and organizing networks. Yet, much of the churches' power has been untapped.

The Industrial Areas Foundation (IAF) was the first network to take seriously the task of developing a powerful community organization within a network of participating parishes and congregations. Other networks have followed. There are nearly two hundred church-based organizations in the country today. Last year the Campaign for Human Development allotted nearly $2.2 million to sixty of them. The goal of church-based organizing is to develop the people's ability to act effectively on issues and values. It builds on both the institutional interest of the parish and the individual interests of clergy and members. One of the tasks of the organizer is to clarify such interests. The organizer encourages leaders to think about how participation in the organization will benefit the church, improving its members' quality of life and building the parish's capacity to act publicly on its own values and teachings.

Biblical and Technological Foundations for Church-Based Organizing

The Catholic Church's support for church-based organizing is grounded in its very definition and mission. The church is a religious institution with a mission in history. In the words of the Second Vatican Council, it is to be "the sign and the safeguard of human dignity." The church must promote social, economic, and political conditions that enhance human dignity and contribute to the common good.

The first stories in the Bible teach that human beings are made in the image and likeness of God, and that the goods of the earth are gifts meant for the benefit of all, not for the advantage of the few. With these God-given gifts goes the responsibility of stewardship. We are to be co-creators with God, working in history to create a society of justice and equity, which enables all to live with the sacred dignity given to them by the Creator.

We also learn about the church's social mission through the life and teaching of Jesus, who used the words of the prophet Isaiah to summarize his own work on earth: "The Spirit of the Lord is upon me, because he anointed me to preach good news to the poor. He has sent me to proclaim release to the captives and to recover sight to the blind, to set at liberty those who are oppressed, to proclaim the acceptable year of the Lord."

Christ's commandment to love our neighbor requires that we both respond to the effects of injustice on an individual's work and to redress the structural causes of injustice lodged in the social, economic, and political institutions perpetuating human suffering. To this end parishes must become effective agents for change. They need to cultivate the skills and the organizational capacity to publicly act on their religious values.

Along with the biblical imperative to work for social change, Catholics are also guided by the teachings of the church's social encyclicals of the past hundred years. They remind us of the significance of human life and human dignity as primary values in the good society. The encyclicals emphatically promote the common good, delineate human rights in the political and economic spheres, and endorse a "preferential option for the poor."

John Paul II has repeatedly urged Christians to practice the virtue of solidarity. He writes, "solidarity is not a vague feeling of compassion or shallow distress at the misfortunes of so many people . . . on the contrary, it is a firm and persevering determination to commit our whole selves to the common good; that is to say, to the good of all and of each individual, because we are really responsible for all."

Guided by the moral vision of the scriptures and the church's social teaching, Catholics have a responsibility to engage in struggles for social and economic justice. When we see poverty, hunger, homelessness, and unemployment in our communities, we understand these social ills to be violations of human dignity. Offensive to the will of God, they challenge us to respond. Church-based organizing is one viable way of responding, a way parishes can practice the virtue of solidarity, participate in the struggle for justice, and work for the protection of human dignity and basic human rights.

For such reasons the U.S. Catholic Bishops created the Campaign for Human Development (CHD). A national collection taken each year in parishes across the nation makes concrete the church's theological teaching. The funds enable low-income families and individuals to determine their own issues, needs, goals, strategies, and organizational vehicles. CHD funding of church-based organizations provides opportunities for low income parishioners to join with those in other religious traditions. Together they work on their issues of concern and put into practice church teachings, their own faith, values, and beliefs.

The Process: Four Stages

While there may be some differences between networks and specific organizing groups, both seem to use a common process in building church-based organizations. There are usually four distinct stages, each built around the developing of relationships. The "one-to-one visit" is essential to every stage of the organizing process. In one-to-one visits the organizer gets to know each person. Such contacts help in assessing individuals' concerns, interests, and readiness to participate in the joint effort; they also build a relationship between the organizer and the individual.

1. Exploration. This period can last two or three years. It involves assessing both the need for and the will within the community to develop a broad-based (city wide/area wide), ethnically diverse, interfaith, multi-issue organization. It requires hundreds of one-to-one visits with local clergypersons, parish and community leaders, diocesan personnel, judicatory heads, and bishops and ordinaries. These sessions include discussions of local problems, the current efforts to address them, and the potential of a larger, more focused organization.

The exploration stage may be initiated by an invitation from a group of local clergy, sometimes called a sponsoring committee, who invite an organizer from a national network to join them. The financial agreements for this stage vary, but may involve a contract to pay the network organizer to do the assessment for a specific number of days per month. In other cases, the exploration period may be initiated by the national network organizer. When a national network considers statewide strategies, some organizations may want to use the occasion to stake out new turf for their group. To circumvent that possibility, the network itself—rather than the local clergy—may opt to initiate the process.

During the exploration stage, the leader draws representatives of local religious bodies together to discuss the organizing project, hear from leaders of church-based organizations in other communities, and plan strategies for expanding participation. The final step is a decision by the sponsoring committee to move ahead or to end the process. If the group decides to proceed, they usually sign a contract with the network to move to a second stage of development.

2. Recruitment. Once a contract has been signed, three things begin to happen. First, at training events for representatives from all the local institutions considering involvement, organizers from national networks share their philosophy, method, and hopes for the community. Afterward, church representatives meet with their parish councils and administrative boards to decide whether they will become a part of the effort. The decision to participate entails paying membership dues. The initial cost for a local church ranges from $500 to $5,000, the exact amount decided by leaders helping to organize the effort.

The recruiting stage may last a year or so, requiring another hundred one-on-one visits from which will emerge local issues of concern. The organizer tries to understand the dynamics of the particular community and helps the organization's leaders think about what might be needed.

Second, the group raises funds from denominational sources (local and national CHD funding, for example) for a three- or four-year organizing drive. One group set a $350,000 goal for the initial four-year organizing phase.

Third, the organizing committee holds another large gathering, perhaps a prayer meeting, bringing together representatives from all the institutions considering joining. Here people meet each other and begin to glimpse the powerful possibilities of working together for a common purpose. The organizers invite bishops, other judicatory leaders, and prominent representatives of nonaligned local congregations whose presence legitimizes and empowers local efforts.

3. Internal parish organization. Once a parish decides to participate and pays its dues, the organizer meets with the clergy, staff, and leaders to determine how they would like to proceed locally. Obviously, what emerges differs with each congregation, depending upon the needs and leaders, but there are some common steps.

Train parish leaders to make one-to-one visits with others in the congregation. The pastor can "send" or "commission" them to go into the community to listen for concerns and to identify others who will join the effort.

Invite those who have been visited to discuss together the issues that have been raised. This group will later decide which issues take priority as they begin their work together. These tend to be both internal parish issues (program for elderly, better liturgies, youth outreach) and external community issues (schools, traffic, housing, and crime).

Using research, find out whether an issue is winnable, what strategies can be used, what funds are available, and who is responsible. Such questions must be answered before moving ahead. Also, develop relationships between leaders within the local organization and decision makers in the city, county, or state. Find allies, identify responsible political leaders, and note possible sources of funding.

Invite large numbers of people to the parish hall for what might be called a "parish assembly meeting," setting the agenda for the next year or two. Those who attend are usually encouraged by the process to become personally involved in one of the selected issues; they may even see such meetings as turning points for their own involvement in parish life. During these "assemblies" the parish may vote to work as well on broader issues of concern to the larger organization.

Internal development depends very much on the local pastor's support. When clergy are not supportive, it is almost impossible to proceed. When they are passively supportive, organizing is possible, but the results will be mixed. When the local clergy see organizing as a helpful strategy to "build the church," these internal steps can be extremely positive. Internal development must not end, however, with the big meeting. Without continued work and follow-through, such efforts could lead to even worse cynicism and frustration. The organizer's ongoing support at this stage is, therefore, crucial.

4. Extension to the broader community. The campaign around a common issue may actually take place while a number of participating institutions are still at step three. It will almost always take place before every parish has completed its internal organizing process. Why? Because an ongoing tension exists between a parish's internal organizing efforts and its external push to establish a new housing program or an improvement of the public school system.

At some point the group must be a focus on the larger issues facing the community. The steps leading to broad-based community actions are no different from those listed earlier: listening first to common concerns coming out of the various congregations; identifying specific issues to be addressed; researching; building relationships; setting specific goals; and bringing together large numbers of people to encourage local officials to act. Gatherings are held to celebrate what has developed in the process of working on issues together. They may involve bishops and other church leaders, include singing and prayer, and remind participants of the common values and teachings that bring them together. If the meeting is a good one, individual members will go home spiritually lifted and moved toward further involvement and participation.

A final step involves careful evaluation of all events and actions. Leaders gather after each event to determine what went right and what went wrong. Individual leaders are encouraged to look carefully at their own performances and to use the evaluation to help them improve in the future. The evaluation may lead to discussions of next steps and further work assignments, new one-on-one visits, and further research.

DETERMINING THE QUALITY OF ORGANIZING EFFORTS

Social action directors question how to determine whether the church-based organizing being done in the parishes is quality work. Such an assessment might involve the following measures:

1. *Is the organization developing both primary and secondary leadership at the parish level?*

One of the criticisms sometimes raised about church-based organizing is that an organizer comes into a parish, works for a while to identify enough good leaders to produce numbers for the big actions, and then moves on to another parish or congregation. The few primary leaders may also become part of the decision-making process for the organization. In a good church-based effort, however, primary leaders are trained and developed on an ongoing basis, through multi-day sessions provided by the national network or in sessions under the auspices of the local organization or a specific parish. Primary leaders will also understand that part of their responsibility is to be recruiting and developing new leaders (sometimes called "secondary leaders") for the parish.

Church-based organizing is criticized when the organizer controls the agenda. The organizer is, of course, a professional, hired to train and advise the leadership of the organization in the best methods for accomplishing its goals. But the organizer may trespass across an invisible boundary, and become the one who determines the organization's direction, leaving the "leaders" to rubber stamp their approval. In a good church-based organization, the leaders (both lay and clergy) make the decisions about which issues to tackle and what strategies to follow. The organizer trains the leaders to accomplish their agenda effectively.

2. Does the organization insure that the leaders move easily between parish and organization leadership roles?

Network representatives often create the expectation that new leaders will be developed for the parish. Our survey showed, in fact, that this is happening. In some cases, though, leaders tend to gravitate toward the organization and away from the parish. Obviously continued deep involvement on both levels can lead to disaster at home, so there may be some periods when the focus is on the organization and other periods when it is on the parish. However, if the trend is away from the parish and never the other way around, the parish involvement in the larger organization must be a means of parish development. Working hard to bring people into the larger issues and struggles of a community will clearly enhance the life of the participating parish community.

3. Is the organization working for a good mix of internal parish development and external issue work?

Some tension will always exist between the internal development of the parish and the common work taken on by the organization as a whole. Recognizing that, one local organization decided to spend every third year focusing on the redevelopment of the local church units. Good organizations understand this tension and work with it. Otherwise, they stand to lose their base of operations; if churches opt out and stop paying dues, the entire effort will fail. Also, it is at the parish level where people begin to learn how to approach issues, become leaders, conduct research, and carry out successful actions. There must be an amenable process of moving from parish, community, or regional issues to joining the leadership team on the larger city-wide efforts.

4. Is the organization inclusive?

Usually the organizational networks are better at this than are parishes. They push parishes to include every religious tradition, every ethnic and racial minority, and to cover the entire city, county, or region. The organizing networks have taught the faith community that it takes all of us to get the results we all want.

5. Is the organization making a real difference on issues in the community?

This is the other side of the "tension" to work within the local congregation. If the organization always focuses on the internal church development and never focuses on the major issues being raised, people will ultimately feel that they have failed to accomplish what the organization was formed to achieve. The organization must become a "player" within the city, county, and state. It must develop the clout to accomplish goals not achievable by the individual parishes. It must be able to point to new school programs, newly built homes, lower crime rates, and safer communities as a result of its group efforts.

6. Does the organization have its own policymaking board or strategy committee?

These boards will differ from organization to organization, but at some point there must be a "strategy team," a board of directors, or some kind of decision-making body. It must decide issues, strategies, actions, and campaigns. The board must also hire and hold accountable the organizing network and the local organizer the network hires. And in an interesting twist the organizer and network, in turn, must hold that group accountable to do the work it plans to do.

7. Does the organization have and/or maintain essential attachments to a national network?

The experience around the country is that unconnected church-based organizations often do not survive long. Somehow the experience of professionals, their distance and objectivity, the accountability they foster, their connections to experiences in other communities, the national training process, and their finding and developing good organizers are very difficult to live without at a local level. Starting a church-based organization that is not a part of one of the national networks (no matter what the experience of the leaders or organizer) is extremely risky. It should only be attempted when no network is available to assist, and even then local groups should affiliate in some way, so they can take advantage of national training sessions and periodic on-site consultation and training.

For the complete text of this paper, contact The Roundtable, 299 Elizabeth Street, New York, NY 10012. Excerpt used with permission.

"The Service of the Poor and Spiritual Growth" by Albert Nolan, OP

Growth in commitment

Our attitude to the poor can grow, develop and mature over the years. On the other hand, it can equally well get stuck and we can become fixed in our relationship to the people we try to serve. For a Christian this is a matter of spiritual growth. Just as there are stages of prayer and stages of growth in love, and just as St. Bernard can speak of steps in the development of the virtue of humility, so also in our commitment to the poor there is an analogous spiritual experience that goes through different steps or stages with its own crises or dark nights and its own discoveries or illuminations.

This article offers an account of these stages of development. It is an account, of course, based partly on my own experience and partly on observation of the experience of others. Moreover, this way of dividing the different stages, like any other division of stages of growth, is inevitably stylized and stereotyped. Others may not experience the stages in the same order or in the same manner. This is a schematization, but offered as an aid to understanding of what takes place in our common journey towards maturity in the service of the poor.

1. Compassion and relief work

The first stage of our commitment to the poor is characterized by *compassion.* We have all been moved personally by what we have seen or heard of the sufferings of the poor. Our experience of compassion has been our starting point. But what I am suggesting is that it is only a starting point and it needs to develop and grow.

Two things help this growth and development of compassion. The first is what we have now come to call *exposure.* The more we are exposed to the sufferings of the poor, the deeper and more lasting does our compassion become. Some agencies these days organize exposure programs and send people off to a Third World country to enable them to see something of the hardships and misery of grinding poverty. Nothing can replace immediate contact with pain and hunger, seeing people in the cold and rain after their houses have been bulldozed, experiencing the unbearable, intolerable smells in a slum, seeing what children look like when they are suffering from malnutrition. But information is also exposure. We know and we want others to know that more than half the world is poor. They say something like 800 million people in the world do not have enough to eat and in one way or another are starving. For many, many people the only experience of life from the day they are born to the day they die is the experience of being hungry. Information of this kind can help us to become more compassionate.

The second thing that seems to me to be necessary to develop our compassion is a *willingness* to allow it to happen. We can put obstacles in the way of this development by becoming more callous, or saying "It's not my business," or "I'm in no position to do anything about it." This blunts one's natural compassion for the sufferings of the poor. As Christians, however, we have a way of allowing our compassion to develop, a way of nourishing our natural feelings of compassion. We believe that compassion is a virtue, a grace and indeed a divine attribute. When I experience compassion I am sharing God's compassion. I am sharing what God feels about the world today.

Moreover, my faith enables me to sharpen and deepen my compassion by enabling me to see the face of Christ in those who are suffering and to remember that whatever we do to the least of his brothers and sisters we do to him. That is powerful.

Compassion leads to *action*. At first our action will probably be what we generally call relief work; collecting and distributing food, blankets, clothes or money. Compassion for the poor might also lead us to a simplification of our lifestyle: trying to do without luxuries, trying to save money and to give our surplus to the poor. I don't want to go into that. There is nothing extraordinary about it; it is part of a long Christian tradition: compassion, almsgiving, voluntary poverty. Much has been said and written about it.

This then would be the first stage, the stage that is characterized by compassion.

2. Discovering structures: the importance of anger

The second stage begins with the gradual discovery that poverty is a *structural problem*. Poverty in the world today is not simply misfortune, bad luck, inevitable, due to laziness or ignorance or a lack of development. Poverty in the world today is the direct result of the political and economic policies of government, parties and big business. In other words, the poverty that we have in the world today is not accidental. It has been created; it has been, one almost wants to say, manufactured, by particular policies and systems. This means that poverty is a political problem, a matter of injustice and oppression.

We have seen that the discovery of the depth and breadth of poverty in the world leads to feelings of compassion. So now the discovery that this poverty is being imposed upon people by unjust structures and policies leads to feelings of *indignation* and anger. We find ourselves getting angry with the rich, with politicians and with governments. We accuse and blame them for their callousness and inhuman policies.

But our Christian upbringing makes us feel somewhat uncomfortable with anger. We feel a little guilty when we get angry with someone. Is it not sinful to be angry? Should we not be more loving towards the rich? Should we not be forgiving the politicians their sins—seventy times seven times? For those of us who want to continue to follow Christ, our anger and indignation can lead us into a deep spiritual crisis.

The way forward and beyond this crisis is bound up with the discovery of the spiritual importance of God's anger. We all know that there is a great deal about God's anger in the bible and not only in the Old Testament. We tend to find this aspect of the bible rather embarrassing and by no means helpful to our spiritual lives. But maybe it is just here that we have something to learn.

There are two kinds of anger and indignation. One is an expression of hatred and selfishness. The other is an expression of love and compassion. God's anger, indeed his wrath, is an expression of his love for the poor *and* for the oppressor. How can that be?

All of us have experienced this kind of anger. When my heart goes out in compassion towards those who suffer, I cannot help feeling angry with those who make them suffer. The deeper my compassion for the poor, the stronger my anger at the rich. The two emotions go together as two sides of the same coin. In fact I cannot experience the one without the other once I know that the rich exploit the poor. And if I have no feelings of anger, or only very little, then my compassion is simply not serious. My anger is an indication of the seriousness of my compassion, just as God's wrath is a sign of the seriousness of his concern for the poor. Unless I can experience something of God's wrath towards oppressors my love and service of the poor will not grow and develop.

And yet God's anger does not mean that he has no love for the rich as persons. We know from experience that we can get angry with the people we love. In fact our anger can be an expression of the seriousness of our love for them. A mother who discovers her child playing with matches and about to burn down the house must get angry with the child. Not because she hates the child but precisely because she loves the child so much. Her anger is an expression of the seriousness of what the child has done and her concern for the child.

Traditionally we distinguish between love of the sinner and

hatred of the sin. This is a notoriously difficult thing to do, but, the more we understand that the problem is unjust structures rather than individuals who can be held personally responsible for poverty, the easier it is to forgive the individual and hate the system. Individuals are only marginally guilty because they are only vaguely aware, if at all, of what they are doing—like the child playing with matches.

As we grow to share more of God's anger, we find our anger directed more at unjust systems than at persons, even if this is sometimes expressed as anger towards those who represent and perpetuate these systems.

That does not mean that our anger becomes weaker. Our compassion can only develop and mature as we learn to take suffering and oppression seriously enough to get really angry about it.

During this second stage, while we are grappling with the structure and systems that create poverty and while we are learning to share God's anger about them, our actions will be somewhat different from the actions we engaged in during the first stage. We will want to change the system. We will want to engage in certain activities that are calculated to bring about social and political change. Relief work deals with symptoms rather than causes. Relief work is like curative medicine as opposed to preventive medicine. What is the point of trying to relieve suffering while the structures that perpetuate the suffering go untouched? Preventive action is political action. And so we find ourselves participating in social actions, supporting campaigns against governments and generally getting involved in politics. This has its own tensions and constraints, especially if you work for the church or for a funding agency or a research institute. But how else can one serve the poor? Relief work is necessary but what about preventive work?

3. Discovering the strength of the poor

The third stage of our spiritual development begins with yet another discovery. It begins with the discovery that the poor must save *themselves* and that the poor will save themselves and that the poor don't really need you or me to save them. Spiritually it is the stage when we come to grips with *humility* in our service to the poor.

Up to now we will have assumed that we must solve the problems of the poor either by bringing them relief or by changing the structures that oppress them. We think that we, the non-poor, the educated and conscientized middle-class, the leaders in the church, the people who work for funding agencies and so forth, must come to the rescue of the poor because they themselves are so pitiably helpless and powerless. There may even be some idea of getting them to cooperate with us. Or there may be some idea of teaching them to help themselves (the classical theory of development). But it is always "we" who are going to teach "them" to help themselves.

The realization that the poor know better than we do what needs to be done and how to do it may come as a surprise. And the further realization that the poor are not only perfectly capable of solving the structural and political problems that beset them but that they alone can do it, may shock and shake us. In spiritual terms this can amount to a real crisis for us and to a very deep conversion.

Suddenly we are faced with the need to learn from the poor instead of teaching them. There are certain important insights and a certain kind of wisdom that we do not have precisely because we are so highly educated and precisely because we are not poor and have no experience of what it means to be oppressed. "Blessed are you, Father, for revealing these things not to the learned and the clever but to the little ones" (Mt 11:25). It takes a considerable amount of humility to listen to and learn from peasants, the working class and the Third World.

When one is dedicated to the service of the poor it is even more difficult to accept that it is not they who need me but I who need them. They can and will save themselves with or without me, but I cannot be liberated without them. In theological terms I have to discover that it is the poor and oppressed who are God's chosen instruments for transforming the world—and not the likes of you and me. God wants to use the poor, in Christ, to save all of us from the madness of a world in which so many people starve in the midst of unimaginable wealth. This discovery can become an experience of God present and acting in the struggles of the poor. Thus we not only see the face of the suffering Christ in the suffering of the poor but also hear the voice of God and see the hands of God and his power in the political struggles of the poor.

Having made this discovery and crossed this hurdle, we open ourselves immediately to a particular kind of *romanticism:* the romanticizing of the poor or of the working class or the Third World.

We Christians seem to have this strange need to romanticize something. Maybe it isn't specific to Christians, but we certainly seem to indulge in it a lot. In the past we tended to romanticize monasticism and then we had this very romantic idea of the missionary who risks everything to save the souls of the pagan savages who live in jungles. We have also tended to romanticize the priesthood and now we are entering a stage of romanticizing the poor.

We romanticize the poor by putting them on a pedestal and hero-worshipping them. We feel that anything that has been said by someone who is poor and oppressed must be true. We listen to people from the Third World as if they possessed some kind of magic, secret knowledge. And whatever the oppressed people of the world do must be right. Any rumor of faults, weaknesses, mistakes and perversities must be rejected out of hand because the poor are our heroes and heroines. This is the kind of romanticism that does the poor and ourselves no good at all. And yet it is extremely difficult to avoid romanticism, at least for a time, during the spiritual development of service to the poor. What matters is that we do eventually grow out of it.

4. From romanticism to real solidarity

The fourth and last stage of development begins with the crisis of *disillusionment* and *disappointment* with the poor. It begins with the discovery that many poor and oppressed people do have faults, do commit sins, do make mistakes, do fail us and let us down or rather fail themselves and sometimes spoil their own cause.

The poor are human beings like any of us. They are sometimes selfish, sometimes lacking in commitment and dedication and sometimes waste money—something that Europeans find particularly irresponsible and incomprehensible. We might even find that some of the poor have more middle-class aspirations than we have and are less conscientized or politicized than we are.

The discovery of these things can be an experience of bitter disillusionment and profound disappointment, a real crisis or dark night of the soul. But it can also be the opportunity for a much deeper and more realistic solidarity with the poor, a conversion from romanticism to realism in our service to the poor.

What we need to remember here is that the problem of poverty is a structural one. The poor are not saints and the rich sinners. Individuals cannot be praised for being poor or blamed for being rich, any more than they can be blamed for being poor and praised for being rich. There are exceptions like those who sell their possessions and embrace voluntary poverty or like those who become rich by exploiting the poor knowingly and intentionally. They can be praised and blamed respectively. But that is not the issue. Most of us find ourselves on one or the other side of the great structural divide of oppressor and oppressed and this has a profound effect upon the way we think and act. It affects the type of mistakes we are likely to make as well as the type of insights we are likely to have. We can learn from the poor precisely because they are not likely to make the same mistakes we are likely to make from our position of education and material comfort. And yet the oppression and deprivation that they might suffer might lead them to have other misunderstandings and misconceptions. We are all conditioned by our place in the unjust structures of our society. We are all alienated by them.

Nevertheless oppression remains a reality. The two sides are not equal. The poor are the ones who are sinned against and who are suffering. Solidarity with them means taking up their cause, not ours. But we need to do this with them. Together we need to take sides against oppression and unjust structures.

Real solidarity begins when it is no longer a matter of "we" and "they." Up to now I have described everything in terms of "we" and "they" because this is how we generally experience the relationship. Even when we romanticize the poor and put them on a pedestal we are alienating ourselves from them. Real solidarity begins when we recognize together the advantages and disadvantages of our different social backgrounds and present realities and the quite different roles that we shall therefore have to play while we commit ourselves together to the struggle against oppression.

This kind of solidarity, however, must be at the service of a much more fundamental solidarity: the solidarity between the poor themselves. Those who are not poor and oppressed but wish to serve the poor and live in solidarity with them often do so in a manner that divides the poor themselves and sets them one against another. We need to find a way of being part of the solidarity that the poor and oppressed are building with one another. After all, we do all have a common enemy—the system and its injustices.

In the end we will find one another in God—whatever our particular approach to God might be. The system is our common enemy because it is first of all the enemy of God. As Christians we will experience this solidarity with one another as a solidarity in Christ, a solidarity with the cause of the poor. It is precisely by recognizing the cause of the poor as God's cause that we can come through the crisis of disillusionment and disappointment with particular poor people.

This is a very high ideal and it would be an illusion to imagine that we could reach it without a long personal struggle that will take us through several stages, through crises, dark nights, shocks and challenges. What matters is that we recognize that we are part of a process. We will always have further to go. We must always remain open to further developments. There are no short cuts. Moreover, we are not the only ones going through this process. Some will be ahead of us and we may grapple to understand them. Others will be only beginning on the road to maturity in this matter. We need to appreciate their process, their need to struggle further and grow spiritually. There is no room here for accusations and recriminations. What we all need is encouragement, support and mutual understanding of the way the Spirit is working in us and through us.

Reprinted with permission from Albert Nolan, OP. Published by Catholic Institute for International Relations, London, England, 1985.

PERSONAL ACTION PLAN

Name: _____ **Daytime Phone:** _____
Parish: _____

A. The Parish

Please assess the degree to which *you* feel the parish meets the following criteria (rate from **1** to **5**, 5 being highest):

1. Liturgy reflects the social mission and teachings of the church. _____
2. Homilies regularly incorporate a social message and challenge the congregation to live out the social message. _____
3. Social Justice is central to religious education and/or Christian formation programs. _____
4. There are opportunities for adult education and participation in the social teachings/mission of the church. _____
5. Prayer is central to your committee's work. _____
6. The parish, as a whole, is generally sensitive to the effect individual church involvement has on other members of the family. _____
7. The parish, and your committee, actively seeks to involve the entire family in programs, projects, sacramental preparation, liturgies, etc. _____
8. The parish is a warm and nurturing place. _____
9. The congregation is involved in the life of the parish. _____
10. People of the parish have ample opportunities to share their spiritual journeys. _____
11. What is the greatest strength of your parish?

    _____
    _____
    _____

12. What is its greatest weakness?

    _____
    _____
    _____

B. Social Concerns Committee

1. Does your parish have an active social concerns committee? _____
    If yes, what is the group called?

    _____

    If no, what is the potential for organizing one?

    _____

    _____

2. Please list under the appropriate heading what types of social ministry
    activities are performed in your parish. Please indicate which fall under
    the auspices of the "social concerns" committee.

Charity & Outreach	Advocacy	Organizing	Solidarity

3. Where is your parish effort in the social mission strongest? Be specific.

    _____

    _____

4. Where is it weakest? Why? _____

    _____

    _____

C. Personal Assessment

1. What are your leadership strengths? _____

   _____

   _____

   Weaknesses? _____

2. How would you describe your preferred style of leadership?

   _____

   _____

   _____

3. Whom do you need to be in relationship with:

   A. to pursue and expand your own areas of interest?

   _____

   _____

   B. to complement your work for a more holistic parish social ministry?

   _____

   _____

D. Action Plan

1. What role would you like to play in developing the social mission of the church in your parish? (Please allow for your own time, energy, limitations, etc.; be realistic.) _____

   _____

   _____

2. State simply and concisely three goals for the next year. They may be personal, professional, and/or parish-based; they may be process or content goals. Under each goal, list three steps necessary to implement each goal. Be specific. By this time next year, I will:

   A. _____

   _____

   B. _____

   _____

   C. _____

   _____

Please list specialized interests (e.g., bereavement, visitation, etc.):

_____

_____

_____

Other follow up: _____

_____

_____

Twenty Key Ideas
"Communities of Salt and Light:
Reflections on the Social Mission of the Parish"

United States Conference of Catholic Bishops, 1994

1. Social Justice is a mission of the whole parish, not a preoccupation of a few (IV,C).
2. Social Ministry . . . is part of what keeps a parish alive and makes it truly Catholic (I).
3. Effective social ministry helps the parish not only do more but be more (I).
4. . . . The local parish is the most important ecclesial setting for sharing and acting on our Catholic Social Heritage (I).
5. A parish's social mission is unique. Nonetheless, it can and should be shaped by our common heritage of Catholic social teaching.
6. The social mission of the parish is never finished. It is a way of life for the entire family of faith. The central message is integrate, don't isolate social ministry.
7. Our social ministry must be anchored in prayer (III, A).
8. The commitment of parishioners to be engaged in the social ministry of the church derives from their actual celebration of the Eucharist. When the link between liturgy and life is clear, the commitment to justice flows naturally.
9. Preaching that reflects the social dimensions of the Gospel is indispensable (III, B).
10. Our social doctrine is an integral part of our faith; we need to pass it on clearly, creatively, and consistently, both in liturgy and through school curriculum and formation (III, B).
11. The most challenging work for justice is not done in church committees, but in the secular world of work, family life and citizenship (III, C).
12. Catholic teaching calls us to serve those in need and to change the structures that deny people their dignity and rights as children of God. Service and action, charity and justice are complementary components of parish social ministry. Neither alone is sufficient; both are essential signs of the gospel at work (III, D).

13. Our parish communities are measured by how they service "the least of these"—the hungry, the homeless, the troubled and the alienated—in our community and beyond (II).

14. Our faith and the Scriptures call us to do more than respond to immediate needs. As individuals and as a faith community, we are called to bring Christ's message of love and justice to bear on the public policies that shape our neighborhoods, our communities, our nation, our world.

15. Parishes need to promote a revived sense of political responsibility calling Catholics to be informed and active citizens, participating in the debate over the values and vision that guide our communities and nation (III, E).

16. Community organizing is an empowerment process that provides a forum for community members to come together to identify problems confronting them and develop effective solutions to those problems.

17. Parishes need to be bridge builders, reminding us that we are part of a Universal Church with ties of faith and humanity to sisters and brothers all over the world. . . . A key test of a parish's Catholicity is its willingness to go beyond its boundaries to serve those in need and work for justice and peace (III, G).

18. The Church teaches that social justice is an integral part of evangelization, a constitutive dimension of preaching the Gospel and an essential part of the Church's mission (II).

19. We need to build local communities of faith where our social teaching is central, not fringe; where social ministry is integral, not optional; where it is the work of every believer, not just the mission of a few committed people and committees (III).

20. The central message is simple—our faith is profoundly social. We realize our own dignity most fully in relationship with others (II).

ENDNOTES

1. Adapted from the Administrative Commission on the Speer Trust, New Castle Presbytery, Presbyterian Church (U.S.A.). Used with permission.

2. We are grateful for the wisdom of Rev. J. Bryan Hehir, as much of this material is adapted from his lectures. Contained in this session also is information from Fred Kammer, SJ, *Doing Faith Justice* (Mahwah, N.J.: Paulist Press, 1991).

3. U.S. Catholic Bishops, "Communities of Salt and Light: Reflections on a Parish Social Mission" (section III, A).

4. Adapted from: Mathis Wackernagel, *Our Ecological Footprint: Reducing Human Impact on Earth* (New Society Publications, 1995).

5. "Communities of Salt and Light," (section III, B).

6. Ibid.

7. Ibid.

8. U.S. Catholic Bishops, *A Century of Catholic Social Teaching: A Common Heritage, A Continuing Challenge*, 1990.

9. John R. Donahue, S.J., "Biblical Perspectives on Justice," *The Faith That Does Justice*, John C. Haughey, ed. (New York: Paulist Press, 1977). p. 69.

10. Section III, C.

11. Hope, Anne, Sally Timmel, and Chris Hodzi. *Training for Transformation*, "Meditation: Development is the New Name for Peace." (Zimbabwe: Mambo Press, 1984.) Book 1, pp. 93–96. Used with permission.

12. Adapted from Henriot, SJ, Pete. *Option for the Poor*, Center of Concern, 3700 13th St., N.E., Washington, D.C. 20017.

13. Adapted from *Training for Transformation*, Book 2 pp. 103–104.

14. "Must We Choose Sides?" Interreligious Task Force on Social Analysis, 1979, pp. 114–115.

15. Justice/Peace Education Council, New York, N.Y.

16. Again, we are grateful for the wisdom of Fred Kammer, SJ, in *Doing Faith Justice*.

17. Adapted from the Naugatuck Valley Project, 63 Prospect Street, Waterbury CT 06702. Used with permission.

18. Adapted from *Doing Faith Justice*.

19. Adapted from a document of the Naugatuck Valley Project, 63 Prospect Street, Waterbury, CT 06702. Used with permission.

20. Adapted materials from: the Study Circles Resource Center, P.O. Box 203, 697A Pomfret Rd., Pomfret, CT 06258; and Barbara Minutillo of the Family Intervention Center in Waterbury, CT. Used with permission.

21. Taken from: Anne Hope, Sally Timmel, and Chris Hodzi. *Training for Transformation*. (Zimbabwe: Mambo Press, 1984.) Book 1, p. 75. Used with permission.

22. Hope, Anne and Sally Timmel. *Training for Transformation*. (Zimbabwe: Mambo Press, 1984.) Book 1, p. 60. Used with permission.

23. Adapted from: Anne Hope, Sally Timmel, and Chris Hodzi. *Training for Transformation*. (Zimbabwe: Mambo Press, 1984.) Book 2, pp. 130–131. Used with permission.